Gazing into Glory
Study Guide

Bruce D. Allen

stillwatersinternationalministries.com abidesinrest@msn.com
Ministry Resources
ISBN-10:0996701400
ISBN-13:978-0-9967014-0-2

Purpose of the Study Guide

This study guide is designed for Christians of any background. Its purpose is to encourage us to reach a greater level of spirituality and help us apply the principles of Gazing into Glory, moving from logos head knowledge to rhema heart experience. Bruce Allen emphasizes that to "gaze into glory" is not just for a select few, but for every child of God. He provides clear instruction on how to "get there." The study guide follows the book closely and attempts to emphasize each step on this adventure, with the purpose of helping us to experience the instruction given in Gazing into Glory, not just read it.

The study guide can be done individually or in groups. Occasionally some additional comments from the CD Album, Gazing into Glory, have been included to provide further insight. Those whose only interaction with the Spirit of God has been prayer, hymns, and church attendance will find a comfortable place to learn in this course. Those who are already experienced in visions or dreams from the Lord will find a mentor in Bruce Allen to help them go even further. Some exercises are for the beginner, while others are for the more advanced.

It is recommended that you do all the exercises, no matter how easy or difficult. Always apply the blood of Jesus. Remember, even the world tells us that practice makes perfect. The Word of God tells us what we focus on, we become (2 Corinthians 3:18). Because of the busyness of our lives, some Focus Cards are included to help you deliberately focus, throughout the day, on the tenets of gazing into glory.

It is our prayer that you would have fresh eyes to see familiar scriptures without old belief systems.

Rev Stan/Nancy Patterson New Beginnings Ministry Salem, SC
newbeginnings888@bellsouth.net

Testimonies can be emailed to Bruce Allen at abidesinrest@msn.com.

Table of Contents
Questions

Answers

Gazing Into Glory

Bruce D. Allen

"My prayer and passion in writing this book is that you, the reader, will enter into your birth-right to see into the realm of the spirit and that you will be activated to walk in that realm regularly."

Preface

1. *Gazing into Glory* is dedicated to those who have a hunger to know the Lord in a more intimate way. Give an example from your life experience that demonstrates your hunger for the Lord.

_____

_____

2. The first century church was filled with power, but today''s church has been overtaken by traditions that have been elevated to take the place of the Word of God. Give an example of man''s tradition replacing the Word. _____

_____.

3. As believers we have access to realms of possibility in the Lord that we have failed to explore through ignorance, fear, or _____.
 (18)

4. Many supernatural manifestations are occurring globally. While we must be circumspect, we must not discard anything of a supernatural nature just because it is outside our personal experience. We must exercise godly _____ and be students of the _____.
 (18)

5. Should you take time to repent? Should a repentance prayer be a daily prayer while studying this book? If so, what would be an example of a repentance prayer?

6. Discernment is not judgment! Discernment is Hebrews 5:14, having our "senses exercised to discern both good and evil." Much of what we have called discernment is

_____.
(19)

7. What two keys in John 14:12 encourage us to seek more interaction with the Spirit realm?
8. a)

_____

b)

_____.
(19)

9. Most people think the greater works (John 14:12) refer to the miracles preformed in the life of Jesus so they covet and desire those same manifestations in their own lives. But there were some "first" works that Jesus walked in that few if any care to emulate. The first works are found in Hebrews 5:7-8. List at least two first works from Hebrews 5:7-8:
a)_____

b)_____
(19)

10. We want the miracles, the signs, and the wonders without the foundation of _____ laid in our lives.
(19)

11. List at least two major points for us to follow in Philippians 2:5-8.
a)

_____

b)

_____
(19)

12. Another first work is found in Philippians 2:7. Jesus *made Himself of no reputation, taking on the form of a* _____.
(20)

13. Many Christians are self-centered and proud with a form of godliness but denying the power thereof by refusing to allow the Holy Spirit to _____ us from our dead works and from the lust of our carnal nature.
(20)

14. What is one thing to be purged from your life? What would be an appropriate prayer for you to pray?

15. In the beginning when Paul came to Corinth, the only way he could effectively communicate to them and see their needs fulfilled was to reach beyond their ignorance of God and their lack of spiritual development by demonstrating the _____ _____ _____.
(21)

16. What is a good prayer to pray, from the model of Paul, when you are around people who are ignorant of God (in question 14)?

17. The anointing and power of God with the nine gifts of the Holy Spirit listed in 1 Corinthians 12 have always been at the basic entry level of the believers" spiritual journey. List the nine gifts of the Spirit:

_____

_____

_____

18. The Lord"s original plan was that signs would follow every believer, not just a select few who have somehow attained a pinnacle of enlightenment. List at least two signs that should follow the believer in Mark 16: 17-18.
a)

_____

b)

_____.

(21)

19. The Lord intended spiritual manifestations to be the normal Christian experience. The supernatural is a starting place for us in our journey to fulfill our destiny on earth, not a stopping place or a camping place. These experiences should become more frequent and more powerful as we _____

_____.

(21)

20. What prayer can be developed from Question 18?

21. Identify some spiritual fruit in your own life.

Introduction

1. Describe the Greco-Roman mindset of the western world.

_____

_____.
(23)

2. Describe the Hebrew mindset.

_____

_____.
(24)

3. What is the desired attitude we should take regarding the Word of God? _____

_____
(24)

4. Explain what Luke 24:45 means to you.

_____

_____.

5. What is a prayer based on Luke 24:45?

6. Explain what Luke 8:9-10 means to you.

_____

_____

7. What is a prayer based on Luke 8:9-10?

Chapter One

Seeing: A Supernaturally Natural Occurrence

1. Spiritual blindness is more incapacitating than _____ blindness.
(27)

2. What is a good prayer to pray about activating your spiritual eyesight (and spiritual hearing)?

3. The ability to "see" in the realm of the Spirit belongs to the select few who have reached the pinnacle of faith. True or False?
(27)

4. Why is it illogical to think that only a few elite can see prophetically with spiritual eyes?
(27-28)

5. Matthew 23:13 says, *But woe unto you scribes and Pharisees, hypocrites for ye shut*
up the kingdom of heaven against men: for ye, neither go in yourselves, neither suffer
ye them that are entering to go in. The Greek word for "go in" literally means "to enter in or to come into." When we don''t understand a scripture, many times, we draw conclusions that are _____ because of unbelief.

6. Once you become born again, can you be in two places at one time? Explain.
(28-29)

7. **Exercise:** Find a quiet place, quiet your mind, and *see* yourself sitting in heavenly places with Jesus. More instruction will be given later on using the sanctified imagination.

8. How have we limited our birthright and our ability to become all the Word says we are?
(29)

9. As we begin to grow spiritually, we use our spiritual senses by:
a) practicing
b) trial and error
c) Both of the above
(29)

10. Why did Jesus speak more about the Kingdom of God than about salvation?
(29)

11. How many scriptures can you find that demonstrate the use of the natural senses (sight, hearing, taste, touch, smell)?

12. Salvation is the entry place to accessing the kingdom of God. Jesus knew that only as we enter and interact with the kingdom of God can we progress in gaining our _____ and ruling as sons and daughters.
(30)

13. The kingdom of God is:
a) within us
b) around us
c) encompasses much more than the natural realm
d) all of the above
(30)

14. Who was created to have dominion over the works of God''s hands?
a) a few spiritual elite
b) all of God''s children
c) scientists
d) none of the above
(31)

15. What is a scripture verse that proves God invested *in us* authority over the works of His hands?
a) Matthew 28:18-19
b) Psalm 8:6
c) both of the above
(31)

16. What are some of the things that have thwarted our spiritual capacity?
a) arrogance
b) ignorance
c) both of the above
(31)

17. What else could thwart our spiritual capacity?
(personal answer)

18. If you eat the Word of God and drink the cup of communion with Him:
a) you are qualified to see with spiritual eyes
b) you are positioned for something you never knew was yours
c) both of the above
(31)

19. What is the "law of first mention?"

_____

_____.

(31)

20. Based upon the law of first mention in Genesis 3, what kind of relationship should we have with God? _____.
(32)

21. BUT! Our relationship with God changed because Adam sinned.
Yes or No
(32)

22. **Exercise:** Based on the example of Jacob in Genesis 28 and Bruce"s revelation,
set your heart and your mind on Christ when you go to bed each night this week.
(33;35)

23. Wherever you go, you can create an atmosphere:
a) with your heart attitude
b) with your voice and your words
c) as you apply the blood of Jesus
d) that releases the atmosphere of heaven
e) that can clean out what has been brought into a place
f) All of the above
(33-34)

24. **Exercise:** Practice creating the atmosphere of heaven wherever you are. A good place to start is at home. Include your work, restaurants you visit, the post office, the grocery store, etc.

25. What is a good prayer to pray for obtaining a face-to-face relationship with God?

26. John 3:3 says, *Jesus answered and said to him, "Most assuredly, I say to you, unless*
one is born again, he cannot _____ *the kingdom of God* and John 10:27 says, *My sheep* _____ *my voice.*
(36)

27. Jesus said, *My sheep hear my voice* (John 10:27). What does the "voice of God"
sound like?
 a) a conviction
 b) a sense of God''s love
 c) pictures or visions
 d) a tangible sense of the presence of God,
 e) audible words
 f) other facets of the "voice of God" that draw us to His side.
 g) All of the above
(36)

28. We have mistakenly thought that God only speaks in words, even though words are the most ineffective form of communication. True or False
(36)

29. In the beginning, when God spoke, a creative force was released, and as a result, everything came into being. We, as sons and daughters of God, who are created in His likeness and image, do not realize the power of our words and what is _____ when we speak!
(37)

30. What God conceived and imagined in His mind, He _____, and then it was created.
(38)

31. So what about negative thoughts or negative images we sometimes see in our mind? Are they sin?
(38)

32. John 3:3 tells us that unless we are born again, we cannot see the Kingdom of God. The word "see" literally and figuratively means to _____.
(38)

33. Is knowing the Lord face-to-face only for Biblical figures? Yes or No
(39-40)

34. John 14:12 says, *Most assuredly, I say to you, he who believes in Me, the works that I do* (not did) *he will do also; and greater works than these he will do, because I go to My Father*. The word "do" is in the continual present tense. What does the continual present tense mean?

_____
(40)

35. How does the continual present tense in John 14:12 make a paradigm shift in your life?

36. Passion is a key to gazing into Glory. Give an example of passion.
(41)

37. Another key to gazing into Glory is _____.
(45)

38. Matthew 5:8 says, *The pure in heart shall _____ God.*
(45)

39. Passion opens the door to _____, as seen in the story of Bartimaeus, who cried out, *"Jesus, Son of David."*
(46)

40. What was the significance of Bartimaeus throwing his cloak off? Why was this important?
(46)

41. What is God calling you to cast off and leave behind?

42. The word "blind" in "blind Bartimaeus" is the Greek word *typhlos,* which means

_____.
(48)

43. One aspect of passion and the desire to "see" the Lord is the willingness to:
  a) surrender our pride
  b) crucify pride at all costs
  c) pay whatever price is necessary to obtain our heart''s desire
  d) All of the above
(48-49)

44. Another key to gazing into Glory is _____.
(49)

19

45. John 14:21 says, *He who has My commandments and keeps them, it is he who loves*
Me. And he who loves Me will be loved by My Father, and I will love him and manifest Myself to him. What is the definition of "manifest?"

_____

_____.

(49)

46. What is a good prayer concerning obedience?
(49)

47. Why have we not embraced the truth of the Lord manifesting Himself to us?
(49-50)
a) Many walk in a powerless gospel which is that is more religious
than relational.
b) We have never been taught that we can "see" the Lord.
c) We are now in a *kairos* moment, a season in which God is revealing
the fullness of His promise.
d) All of the above.

48. John 14:13 says, *Whatever you ask in my name, that will I do because I go to the*
Father. The meaning of the word "name" in this verse is:
(50-51)
a) the name Jesus was given at birth
b) character, honor, authority
c) both of the above

49. What is Bruce''s paraphrase of John 14:13?
(50-51)

50. Matthew 18:20 says, *Where two or three are gathered in my name, I am there in the*
 midst of them. Paraphrase this verse using the correct meaning of "name."
(50-51)

51. From the example of Pastor Glen, what is a good prayer to pray?
(55)

Chapter Two
Seeing: A Face-to-Face Reality

1. What may be the most important question for you in Chapter Two, found on page 57?

_____.

(57)

2. What should John 8:38 do to our faith? John 8:38 - *I speak what I''ve seen with my Father*.

_____

_____

_____.

(57)

3. What does John 1:51 say to us? John 1:51 - *Most assuredly I say unto you, hereafter you shall see Heaven open and the angels of God ascending and descending*
upon the son of man.

_____

_____

_____.

(57)

4. What is the insight we have overlooked Acts 1:11?
Acts 1:11 - *Men of Galilee, why do you stand gazing up into Heaven, the same Jesus*
who was taken up from you into Heaven will so come in like manner as you saw him go into heaven.
(58)

5. What is the insight we have overlooked in Isaiah 6:1?
Isaiah 6:1 - *In the year that King Uzziah died, I saw the Lord sitting on a throne, high and lifted up, and the train of His robe filled the temple.*
(59)

22226. If our eyes are opened, and we walk in the fullness of our supernatural birthright, the major issue we will have to deal with is:
(59)
a) pride
b) persecution
c) discernment
d) None of the above

7. Character is revealed, not formed, through tests and trials. True or False
(59)

8. What test did Uzziah fail?
(59)

9. It is our birthright to see and to know Him face-to-face. One key is passion. Hindrances can be pride, ignorance, tradition, and _____ of men instead of the Word of God.
(60

10. What is the insight we have missed in the story of the prodigal son?
(61-64)

11. If you want more anointing and revelation, what must you do?
(62)

12. Seedtime and harvest have never been exclusively about _____. They are about planting and giving away your anointing and revelation. In time you will reap more back to yourself.
(62)

13. If you and I do not share our anointing and revelation, we will experience a spiritual famine by:
a) wasting our inheritance among ourselves (the church)
b) becoming tempted to compromise with the world
c) eating whatever the world feeds us
d) All of the above
(62)

14. The revelation that came to the prodigal son through brokenness and humility was seen in the shift in attitude from "give me" to "_____ _____."
(63)

15. Is there someone in your family (or life) who fits the description of "grossly immature, backslidden in heart, or lost?" Based on this insight, what new prayer would you pray for that person?

16. Accepting responsibility for one"s own actions is a sign of

_____.
(63)

17. The purpose of our life is: (select all that apply)
(64)
a) becoming like Jesus
b) worshipping God by obedience to His Word
c) doing good works
d) feeding the poor

18. What are we to focus on according to 2 Corinthians 4:17-18?
_____.
(64)

19. How can we look at and see the things that are not seen? How can we see the invisible?

_____

_____.
(64)

20.Since spiritual blindness more incapacitating that physical blindness, how do we overcome spiritual blindness?
(65)

21. What are other ways to connect spiritually besides seeing?

(65)

22. In the same way we connect through our five senses physically, we can connect both visually, by scent, by hearing, by touch and by taste with the Spirit realm. It is essential, even imperative, that we learn to utilize and function with our spiritual senses. Have you experienced a touch, an audible word, a fragrance, a vision, or a taste of the Lord?

23. The word "see" in John 3:3 *(Truly, truly I say unto you; except a man be born again, he cannot see the kingdom of God)* literally means _____. What does this mean to us?
(66)

24. In Luke 24:13 two disciples are traveling on the third day to a city called Emmaus, which was literally a distance of 7½ miles from Jerusalem. What is the significance of the number 7½?
(66-67)

25. The road to Emmaus is a prophetic picture of the body of Christ, early in the _____ of the third day after the resurrection.
(67)

26. As we make the choice to journey or move toward this place of consistent passion, Jesus himself comes alongside us and begins to open the Word to us. True or False?
(67)

27. When the disciples reached Emmaus, what was the key to their eyes being opened to recognize Jesus?
(67)

28. Mark 9:2 says, *Now after six days Jesus took Peter, James, and John, and led them*
up on a high mountain apart by themselves; and He was transfigured before them.
"After six days" means the seventh day. Explain how we are living in the seventh day.
(68)

29. What is the significance of the seventh day?
(68)
18

30. We have made prayer a religious byword rather than a time of visiting with our heavenly Father. How should we improve our prayer life?
(69)

31. What is the Hebrew oral tradition about Jesus and his prayer time?
(69)

32. What is another scripture that verifies our birthright to see the kingdom of God?
(69)

33. BUT! Exodus 33:20 says, *But He said, „You cannot see My face; for no man shall*
see Me, and live." How does 2 Corinthians 5:17 answer this objection?
(70)

34. 1 Timothy 6:15-16 says, *Which He will manifest in His own time, He who is the blessed and only Potentate, the King of kings and Lord of lords, who alone has immortality, dwelling in unapproachable light, whom no man has seen or can see, to*
whom be honor and everlasting power. Amen. What is the definition of "man" who cannot see the Lord?
(70)

35. List a scripture from the Old Testament that verifies a relationship with the Lord that is face-to-face.
(70)

36. In Mark 9:1-7, the story of the transfiguration, Jesus talked to Moses and Elijah _____ to _____, beyond the veil of eternity.
(71)

37. On many occasions Bruce has seen into the realm of the spirit and witnessed the operation of the Spirit of God, the angelic, the demonic and also the human spirit. Describe what he saw as our human spirit.
(72)

38. What darkens the light that is within us?
(72)

39. Describe the vision Bruce's friend had on the airplane.
(72)

40. The vision emphasized that we have neglected our own responsibility to
_____ ourselves and work out our own salvation with fear and
trembling.
(72)

41. A sign of maturity is accepting responsibility for our own actions.
But what are we, like Adam, quick to do?
(73)

42. When Jesus was talking to Moses and Elijah in Mark 9, was he going against
scripture in Deuteronomy 18:10-12, about not talking with the dead?
(73-74)

43. Explain the difference between those who have accepted Christ and are *alive*
in Him (though *asleep* in the grave) and those who have not accepted Christ
and are *dead*.
(74)

44. How is it that Peter, James, and John recognized Moses and Elijah?
(75)

45. Which of the following is true about revelation and visitation?
(75-76)

a) Visitation always brings revelation.
b) Revelation can come without visitation.
c) When visitation and revelation come together, a person (or group)
is changed from that moment on and activated into a new realm on
insight and intimacy.
d) All of the above

46. Jeremiah 12:5 says, *If you have run with the footmen, and they have wearied
you,*
then how can you contend with horses? What is the meaning of this verse?
(76)

47. What is a definition of the Glory?
(77)

48. What does the word "see" mean in John 1:51? *(Most assuredly I say to you, hereafter you shall see heaven open, and the angels of God ascending and descending*
upon the Son of Man.)
(77)

49. You are the body of Christ; angelic encounters should be a normal Christian experience, not the exception. What is the word of caution regarding angelic encounters?
(77)

50. Bruce sometimes sees the angel assigned to churches he visits. Describe two conditions of these angels he has seen and what that means.
(77-78)

51. Only people considered to be spiritual giants have visions and see angels. True or False?
(78)

52. When should we expect the return of the Lord?
a) pre-tribulation
b) mid-tribulation
c) post-tribulation
d) today
(80)

53. Visions are _____, as is the spoken word.
(81)

54. Will you pray the prayer at the end of Chapter Two?

Chapter Three
The Sanctified Imagination: Eyes on Him

1. Based on Chapter Two, what is now your focus?

2. Matthew 5:28 says, *I say unto you whoever looks on a woman to lust after her has committed adultery with her already in his heart.* What does this verse imply about our imagination?
(85)

3. What is the difference between unclean thoughts and unclean meditations?
(86)

4. What is the major battlefield where our enemy fights against us?
(86)

5. Most of us understand that our mind is the battleground of the enemy. He will batter you with thoughts all day long. Some have no victories because they don''t understand this battleground. Some have had a few victories but are growing weary in well doing and fighting the good fight of faith. To increase our victories, we should realize that the fight of faith is an inward understanding and a tenacious standing on the Word of God. That is why Paul admonishes us to take every thought _____ to the obedience of Christ in 2 Corinthians 10:5.
(86)

6. How do YOU apply 2 Corinthians 10:5?

_____

_____.

7. Ephesians 1:17-19 - *That the God of our Lord Jesus Christ, the Father of glory may*
give unto you the spirit of revelation in the knowledge of Him. The eyes of your
understanding being enlightened, that you may know what is the hope of His calling
and what the riches of the glory of His inheritance in the saints, and what is the
exceeding greatness of His power to us who believe according to the working of His
mighty power. What are the eyes of our understanding?
(86-87)

8. What are the two basic Greek words that deal with the word "mind" in the New Testament?
(87-89)

9. The first word for "mind" is *dianoya* (Strong"s #1271), which means

_____.

What verse contains this word?
(87)

10. What is a good paraphrase of Matthew 22:37?
(87)

11. How do we love the Lord with our imagination?
(87)

12. **Exercise:** Close your eyes and picture yourself in a certain location, like a beach or mountain, with details surrounding you as listed on page 87. Share with the group at least one statement about your experience with this exercise.
(88)

13. What is our answer to those who say meditation is of the devil?
(88)

14. What does *The New Dictionary of Theology,* Volume 3 say about *dianoya?*
(88)

15. What does *Vine"s* dictionary say about *dianoya?*
(88)

16. So... will you believe the world about meditation or will you obey God"s instruction to meditate?

17. The second word for "mind" is *dialogisimo* and it means, literally, "to _____ _____, to deliberate by reflection (Strong"s #1260). It speaks of a logical, reasoning, mind. What verse contains this word?
88)

18. What hinders our spiritual growth and ability to walk in revelation and intimacy available to us through the cross?
(88)

19. We must _____ our logical minds and our imagination.
(88)

20. The devil wants you to misunderstand the use and power of your sanctified imagination. He does not want you to gain insight and revelation concerning the eyes of your understanding or your imagination. He does not want the eyes of your *dianoya* (imagination) to be enlightened because _____

_____.
(89)

21. Discuss the example given by Bruce when he prayed for a particular person"s healing. How do we apply this to ourselves?
(89-90)

22. Explain the connection between the mind, the heart, and the Spirit.
(90)

23. **Exercise:** In groups of three, pray for any healing needed for each person.

Help the person receiving the prayer to visualize himself/herself correctly, after the prayer.

24. **Review:** The western church has been concerned with: (select correct answers)
a) *dianoya* or strong imagination
b) *dialogisimo* or strong logical mind
c) a Greek mindset or needing to understand how God can do
(90,24)
something before believing He can do it
d) a Hebrew mindset or believing God can do what He says, without understanding how He can do it

25. To doubt with the heart means to doubt with the

_____.
(90)

26. The Greek word for "enlightened" in Ephesians 1:18 is *fotitsmo* (Strong"s #5461). What English word do we derive from *fotitsmo?*
(90)

27. Elaborate on the eyes of your understanding and the word *fotitsmo.*

28. Explain two steps Bruce uses to sets his affections on things above.
(91)

29. There is a biblical principle that states: what you focus on, you will
_____ with and when connection comes, _____
takes
place.
(91)

30. What does "activation"
mean?_____.
(91)

31. What scripture contains this principle of becoming what you focus on?

32. What is Bruce"s paraphrase of Ephesians 1:18?

_____

_____.

(91)

33. What is YOUR paraphrase of Ephesians

1:18?_____ _____

_____.

34. What creates a bridge between the soul and spirit?

(91)

35. As we begin to exercise and practice sanctifying our thought life and framing pictures of the kingdom of God in our imaginations, what happens?

_____

(91)

36. The more we practice this new language of pictures of the Kingdom of God, the more fluent we become in this language, and the more fluent we become, the quicker the activation comes. True or False

37. The Hebrew word for "meditate" in Joshua 1:8 is *haga* (Strong"s #1897). What is the meaning of *haga*?

(92)

38. What does Joshua 1:8 tell us about meditation?

_____

(Bible)

39. **Review:** What is the Greek word for "meditate" in 1 Timothy 4:15, and what does it mean?

(92)

40. Paraphrase 1 Timothy 4:14-15 using the Greek meaning of "meditate."

41. The result of giving ourselves wholly to imagining or framing pictures in our mind of heavenly principles, beings, or activities is that we will prosper and it will be obvious to all, as in the example of Brother Lawrence and Frank Laubach. True or False

42. **Exercise:** Place yourself in Mark 1:40-41, the cleansing of the leper. Imagine yourself standing beside Jesus when the leper came to Him. Hear the request and Jesus" answer. Imagine what the former leper said and did when he was healed. Imagine the details of the scene. Was a breeze blowing that day? OR imagine yourself to be the leper coming to Jesus and receiving healing.

43. Discuss Bruce"s experience of overcoming shyness, practicing preaching, and imagining miracles, including his battle with Satan.
(93-94)

44. What does Hosea 4:6 say about lack of knowledge?
_____
(We are gaining knowledge about meditation as a tool for the kingdom.)
(93-94)

45. Genesis 11:6 says: ...*and now nothing will be restrained from them, which they have*
_____ *to do.*
(95)

46. Does Genesis 11:6 mean that if we (the body of Christ) are in unity, and imagine the same objective, we will receive that which we are seeking and focusing on?   Yes or no
(95)

47. Can you give another scripture to verify Genesis 11:6?
(95)

48. John 8:56 says: *Your father, Abraham, rejoiced to see my day: and he saw it, and*
was glad. Both the word „see" and „saw" are the Greek word *edio* (Strong"s #1492), which means
_____ .

49. Give another scripture that verifies that by faith we can see the future.
(96)

50. Hebrews 11:27 says, *By faith he (Moses) forsook Egypt, not fearing the wrath of the*
king: for he endured, as _____ *him who is invisible.* "Seeing" in this verse
is *horao,* which means "to stare at." Moses developed a relationship with the
Lord, as seeing Him who is invisible.
(96)

51. What are two keys Bruce has found to seeing the invisible?
(96)

52. Isaiah 26:3 says, *You will keep him in perfect peace, whose* _____ *is stayed*
on thee: because he trusts in thee. The Hebrew word *yetser* (Strong"s #3336) means
mind and speaks of _____.
(96)

53. Paraphrase Isaiah 26:3.

54. What are other scriptures to which this insight brings new significance?
(96)

55. How to we learn to see something invisible?
a) Begin with your sanctified imagination.
b) Keep your mind stayed on Him (Isaiah 26:3)
c) Persevere with passion because this is a process.
d) All of the above.

56. Our first step in starting this new adventure with the Lord in "seeing" is to
step out of _____ .
(96)

57. This chapter has been a discussion on the sanctified imagination. Give an
example of an unsanctified imagination.

Dr. Bruce D. Allen

Chapter Four
The Sanctified Imagination: Activating Adventure

Whatever you focus on, you connect with, and activation will take place.

1. If we practice the tools in *Gazing into Glory,* instead of just reading about them, our lives will be drastically changed, and our journey with the Lord will become an adventure. True or False
(99)

2. Discuss Bruce's example of the man who "met" with Jesus every day by framing a picture of Jesus in his mind, and talking to Jesus as if He were there in person.
(99-101)

3. **Exercise:** Practice this tool for five minutes each day this week. Go to a quiet place and focus your heart and mind on Jesus, visualizing or framing a picture of Him in front of you. If five minutes is too difficult, try three minutes, or at least one minute. Report your results at the end of one week. Decide if you want to practice this exercise more than one week.

4. Most of us can stay focused on one thing for eight to ten minutes.
    True or False

(101)
5. As you begin to discipline your mind to focus on one thing,
a) other thoughts will enter your mind and try to distract you.
b) cast distracting thoughts down (2 Corinthians 10:5).
c) persist and remember you cannot undo the undisciplined mind in one day because you have experienced it for most of your life.
d) keep practicing and you will activate what you are focusing on.
e) have a passion to experience God, not just hear about Him.
f)) All of the above

6. The bridge from the natural realm to the supernatural realm is a

_____.

(102)

7. What experience brought the scriptures to life for Bruce? How can you receive this experience?
(102)

8. What was Bruce''s example of "taking" his land from the devil, since he fell asleep every time he read the Bible in the early days?
(102)

9. Discuss Bruce''s attitude of "I want that" and what 2 Corinthians 12:2 and Jeremiah 1:5 meant to him.
(103-104)

10. One principle Bruce has learned is that once he has had an experience with the Lord, he can _____ that experience anytime.
(106)

11. What daily discipline did Bruce follow to increase in the ability to see with a sanctified imagination? What are you willing to commit to?
(106)

12. **Exercise:** You focused for five minutes in the last exercise. Now, for ten minutes, focus on a framed picture of Jesus in your imagination. Share your experience or your difficulty.

13. What is the rule to follow from 1 John 4:2-3?
(107)

14. In the example about tuning a radio dial, what is the application for us?
(108-109)

15. Give one reason why it is important to pray in tongues and discuss the example from the Gazing into Glory Conference in Tum Tum, Washington.
(109-112)

16. A natural outflow of our relationship with Him is the ministry in our lives of His _____.
(112)

17. Proverbs 6:16-19 says, *These six things doth the Lord hate: yea, seven are an abomination unto him: A proud look, a lying tongue, and hands that shed innocent blood, An heart that deviseth wicked _____, feet that be swift in running to mischief, a false witness that speaketh lies, and he that soweth discord among brethren.*
(112)

18. Why does the Lord hate wicked imaginations?
(113)

19. Discuss the example of what not to do, given by the young man who became focused on Adolf Hitler.
(113)
33

Dr. Bruce D. Allen

Chapter Five
Walking the Talk

The bridge between the natural and the supernatural is a sanctified imagination.

1. Which scripture tells us what to think?
(115)

2. **Review:** What is the bridge between the natural and the supernatural?
(115)

3. Our standard for living and for our focus is always the _____ of God. As we frame pictures properly in our imagination of the kingdom of God, eventually we will connect with the kingdom, and our eyes will be opened.
(116)

4. We start with the Word and end with the Word. In between we _____ the Word of God in our lives, and something transpires that causes us to come into a new realm of intimacy and revelation with God. When we do this, God will bring us to a place of destiny and our inheritance.
(116)

5. *Gazing into Glory* is a compilation of the tools and revelation God gave to Bruce Allen over a number of years. If we apply them to our lives, and step out of religion and the doctrines of man, we will experience_____ in connecting with the spiritual world, so that it will only take us hours, days or months, instead of years.
(116)

6. Hebrews 5:13 says: *For everyone that uses milk is unskillful in the word of righteousness for he is a babe. But strong meat belongs to them that are of full age, even those who by reason of use have their senses exercised to discern both*
(116)
good and evil. The word "exercise" literally means _____ .

7. Paraphrase Hebrews 5:13 using the correct meaning of "exercise."

8. What are our senses?
(116)

9. Have you ever "sensed" the supernatural atmosphere in a room?
(116-117)

10. Discuss the example in the book about "touching" in the spirit. Have you felt a physical "touch" that you can share?
(117-118)

11. In the story of the pastor who touched angels, what was significant about using the left hand if one were right handed, or vice versa?
(118)

12. Colossians 1:21 says, *And you who once were alienated and enemies in your mind*
(imagination) *by wicked works, yet now he has reconciled.* How are we an enemy of God in our imagination?
(119)

13. Sometimes we glibly quote scriptures like "*I have the mind of Christ*" or "*Nothing is impossible.*" Just quoting the Word, without _____ and _____is dead works. We must apply the Word by what we think, what we speak, and what we do so that it becomes a reality in us and through us.
(119)

14. The first and great commandment is Matthew 22:37 "*Jesus said to him, you shall love the Lord your God with all your heart, with all your soul, and with all your*
mind (imagination, *dianoya*). The first commandment with promise is to love the Lord your God with all your imagination. How do we do that?
(120)

15. Luke 12:29 (NKJV) says, *Do not seek what you should eat or what you should drink, nor have an anxious mind* (imagination). What is an "anxious" mind or imagination?
(120)

16. When we read newspapers, books, the Bible, pictures are _____ in our imagination. We must learn to "frame" right images within our imaginations at all times.
(120)

17. Once we are redeemed, if we continue to allow our imaginations to revisit and dwell upon anything that is unclean and contrary to scripture, we once again fulfill the desires of the imagination and come under the curse of the children who are subject to _____. An unsanctified imagination wanders anywhere it wants to go.
(121)

18. What is another scripture about imagination?
(121)

19. What is the name of a famous person who exercised a sanctified imagination, practicing the presence of God?
(121-122)
 face, as a friend, just as Moses did?"
(122)

21. Would you like to be known in your area as the person who knows God face-to-face? Yes or No
 37

22. **Exercise:** Whatever Brother Lawrence was doing, all day long, his heart and mind were focused on Jesus. Take five minutes, as you go about your day, and focus on Jesus. Don"t get discouraged if your mind wanders. You are practicing.

23. **Exercise Advanced:** Fix your heart and imagination on God. If you start to see a vision, stop! Make yourself focus again on the natural realm instead of the spiritual realm. Then go back to focusing on the vision. The point is that the spiritual realm is eternal and without time, so you can return to your vision anytime.
(122-123)

24. We will get to the place where every time we come before the Lord, we will literally be before His throne, because we persist and continue to exercise our senses. What does it mean to exercise your senses by "reason of use?"
(122-123)

25. It is time to make a decision. If your present level of interacting with the Spirit is the limit of where you want to be with the Lord, then it is time to stop this course. If you want to press on, like saints of history, like Brother Lawrence, then continue with this course. What is your decision? (Read the answer for help making this decision.)
(123)

26. Ambassadors are supported by their own country, even when they are visitors in a foreign country. The government they represent pays for every expense incurred. When they return home, they do not have to go through the screening of ordinary people. We ourselves are ambassadors of _____ _____ .
(124)

27. Since we are citizens of heaven, and Jesus opens and closes doors for us, as His ambassadors, we can also return home on furlough. Where does it say in the Word that we can visit heaven?
(124-125)

28. **Exercise:** Explain what we have considered to be the meaning of the scripture John 14:12, that we will do the same or greater works than Jesus does. Explain what Jesus is doing now that we should therefore be doing.
(124-125)

29. **Review Exercise:** Use a stopwatch. Actually record how many seconds you are able to focus on Jesus before your mind wanders. How long were you able to focus?
(125)

30. Discipline and focus are keys to gazing into glory. The concept of the mind _____ the Spirit is very important. This is how the mind (imagination) is used to help you connect to the realm of the Spirit; it builds the bridge. We should focus on the Lord every time we worship or pray. Practice. Focus on

the Lord and the things of the Spirit. Keep on practicing. Keep on focusing on the Lord and the things of the Spirit. *This is how the mind (imagination) is used to help you connect to the realm of the Spirit by building a bridge from your mind to the supernatural.*
(125)

31. Describe Bruce''s experience with a portal in the chair of his friend. Have you ever experienced a portal?
(126-128)

32. In that experience, Bruce asked the Lord to show him where the vision was in the Word. An experience without a biblical basis is a _____. If you have a vision, take time to meditate on it and get in the Word of God concerning; then you can prove if it is real or not.
(127)

33. Where is the law of first mention with regard to a portal?
(128)

34. Name at least two things that cloud our perspective and block our spiritual eyesight.
(128)

35. **Exercise (again) Practice Focusing:** Close your eyes; ask the Holy Spirit to help you frame a picture of Jesus, and focus. Focus as long as you can before your mind wanders.
(125, 129-131)

36. **Exercise:** Imagine yourself seated in heavenly places with Christ. Remember we are created to be in two places at once. See yourself looking down at your present circumstance and conversation. The heavenly place where you are seated may be in your back yard, as in heaven on earth. (This exercise is also to be done many times throughout the day, every day.)

37. Why was it important for the man whose language with God included twitching fingers to not talk about his twitching fingers, but to just talk about what the Lord was saying?
(129)

38. Joshua 3:2 gives instruction to "_____ yourselves, for tomorrow the

LORD will do wonders among you."
(130)

39. The word for "transformed" in Romans 12:2 is the same word used in Mark 9:2 where it speaks of Jesus being "transfigured" before the disciples. It is *metamorpho* (Strong"s#3339) and means _____.

40. **Exercise:** Follow Bruce"s example from the section Looking in the Mirror and see yourself transformed into the image of Christ, daily. Find a mirror to aid in this exercise.
40

Chapter Six
The Living Body of Christ

1. What is the prayer Bruce prays every night?
(133)

2. What was the prophetic word he received confirming that prayer? How might this apply to your life?
(133-134)

3. Discuss Bruce"s visit to the Throne Room of God when he was in Belfast, including his answer when the Lord extended His scepter. Compare Bruce"s answer and Pastor Glenn"s answer in Chapter One, when a scepter was also extended.
(134-136)

4. Is it acceptable to bring our petitions to the Lord? (yes or no) What is the more desirable position, rather than bringing our petitions?
(137)

5. What were some insights Bruce gleaned from that experience?
(137)

6. Discuss what Bruce experienced that was released to the Body of Christ.
(138)
Include "Make me" replacing "Give me."

7. Our "members" literally means our "senses." Paraphrase Romans 6:13.
(138)

8. What prayer based on Romans 6:13 could be added to your arsenal of daily weapons?
(138)

9. **Review:** The Hebrew word for "mind" in Isaiah 26:3 is *yester,* which means "that which is formed in the imagination." Paraphrase Isaiah 26:3 to include this literal meaning.
(139)

10.   There is a connection between heart _____ and spiritual sensitivity in the scriptures.
(139)

11. The battleground is internal and has to do with discipline in your mind and thought life, and lining up the thought life with the will of God, the purposes of God, and the Word of God. True or False
(139)

12. But how can I ever be pure in heart with the things done in my past?
(139-140)

13. But isn"t it in heaven when the pure in heart see God?
(140)

14. The Greek word for "see" in Matthew 5:8 *(Blessed are the pure in heart for they*
shall see God) is *optanomai*, which means

_____.
(140)

15. We get our word _____ from *optanomai*. This means we are putting
on a lens or "spiritual glasses" which enables us to gaze with wide open eyes at something that is remarkable.
(140)

16. Proverbs 22:11 says, *He who loves _____ of heart and has*
_____ on his
lips, the king will be his friend.
(140-141)

17. What four keys does Bruce encourage us to implement so we will gain a face-to-face relationship with the Lord?
(141)
42

18. Discuss Bruce''s experience while in Kirkland, WA, seeing Jesus in a pillar of fire.
(141-144)

19. I John 4:17 says, ...*As He is, so are we in this world.* Not "as He was," but "as He
is", and He is _____. Instead of desiring His gifts, we should earnestly desire to be like Him.
(144)

20. What verse tells us to first give our heart to Him, and then we will observe His ways?
(144)

21. What is the heart?

(145)

22. The scripture verse, 2 Corinthians 3:18, tells we will be changed as we focus on God.   True or False
(145-146)

23. Instead of praying, "Lord, I want to do this and that," it is better to pray, "Lord, what do You want? What are You doing today? I want to be part of what You are doing." True or False

24. Reminder: We become what we focus on. What is one scripture regarding this principle?
(145-146)

25. Discuss "Holy Meditation." Include our wrong teaching, why and how to meditate, using Bruce''s example of 2 Corinthians 3:18.
(146)

26. What is the meaning of "meditate?"
(146)

27. Discuss how 1 Corinthians 15:49 *(We have borne the image of the man of dust, we shall also bare the image of the heavenly man)* and 2 Corinthians 3:18 (Beholding as in a mirror the Glory of the Lord) are keys to interacting with the heavenly realm.
(148-149)

28. When you look to the Lord with the eyes of your heart, and you begin to see yourself in the mirror being transformed in His image, a divine _____ takes place. *This is key to interacting with the heavenly realm.*
(148)

29. **Exercise:** *Beholding as in a mirror the glory of the Lord.* Find a mirror and gaze into your reflection for five minutes, seeing the reflection of Jesus in your face. Share your experience. As you practice this daily at home, increase the time you are gazing into the mirror.
(148)

30. What you focus upon you will become like through impartation. The end result of an unsanctified imagination is clearly shown in Romans 1:21 *(Because when they knew God, they glorified Him not as God, neither were thankful, but became vain in their imaginations and their foolish heart was darkened.)* If we don"t learn to harness our imagination, our hearts will be_____through vain imaginations.
(148)

31. Enoch was translated. What was his secret to attaining this position with God?
(149)

32. If we truly believed the Word, we would live differently and act differently. The veil of _____ is the first to go, but as you begin this process more veils begin to fall away, and the more this happens, the clearer the image will become, and the clearer the image becomes, the greater the manifestation of *Christ in you, the hope of glory* (Colossians 1:27).
(150-151)

33. **Exercise:** *Position-ally*, every promise in the Bible is ours. *Possession-ally*, we don"t walk in this truth. Is there a promise given you by the Lord that you have not walked in because of unbelief? If so, what are you going to do about it?
(150)

34. *One day is as a thousand years with God* (2 Peter 3:8). From the time of Jesus to
the turn of the century, we have completed two thousand years, or two days, so now we find ourselves early in the morning on the 3rd day. From the time of Adam to the turn of the century, we have completed six days and now we are early in the morning on the _____ day.

(151)
 (Recommended reading: *Promise of the Third Day* and *The Prophetic Promise of the Seventh Day* by Bruce D. Allen.)

35. On this seventh day we are an Enoch generation. We can walk with God and be transferred just as he was because the Lord is no respecter of persons! What is the possibility of God in *your* life? What are *you* believing God for? Where is your heart fixed?

36. Image clarity has to do with purity of heart. It has to do also with proficiency, which comes through _____.
(151)

37. Discuss Bruce''s experience in Fiji when he was sick and the three children got healed "rolling" in his bed and were healed after he left.
(152)

38. Discuss the experience of the minister getting a massage when he consciously released the anointing.
(153-154)

39. **Exercise:** Picture yourself daily so immersed in God, that everywhere you walk, there is a release of the anointing or Glory of God that is resident upon you, and anyone who comes close to you is affected by that radiance, everywhere you go. Practice consciously releasing the anointing.
(152-153)

40. As every veil of unbelief melts away, clarity of the Kingdom of God becomes more and more _____.
(154)

41. Give at least one scripture about what we focus on coming out of our heart, our mouth, or our view of life.
(154)

42. Discuss the experience of demons fleeing from Bruce and Reshma in Belfast. What is the Biblical example?
(154-156)

43. **Practice, practice, practice.** If you will begin to practice keeping your focus on Jesus by meditating, imaging and pursuing Him, you will be awakened to a capacity of sight you never knew was available to you. Remember, what you focus on, you will connect with. Once connection comes, activation takes place!
46

Chapter Seven
Translation by Faith: Getting Ready

1. What is translation?
(159)

2. Bruce"s teaching on translation is based on both experience and the Word of God. True or False
(159)

3. The Spirit and the Word have to come together to bring clarity. The scriptural basis in the Old Testament is the story of Enoch. What is the scriptural basis in the New Testament for translation?
(159)

4. How do we prepare to be translated?
(160)

5. Give the account of how Bruce came to translation by faith.
(159-163)

6. What are the two phases of this revelation, in Bruce"s teaching?
(161-162)

7. What is the experience of translation by the pastor in Russia?
(162)

8. Discuss the experience of Richard from Kenya.
(162-163)

9. **Review:** Why does mainstream Christianity have difficulty believing in the supernatural?
(163)

10. **Review:** What is the key verse about our doing the works, and even greater works, of Jesus?
(163)

11. Discuss the section titled Walking by Faith, especially concerning the greater works. Include John 6:15-21 (immediately reaching shore, 3 ½ miles away) and Acts 12:5-11 (Peter being freed from prison).
(163-166)

12. The testimony of Brother Grubbs challenges our faith. What is a good prayer to pray for believing the Lord for the fullness of our inheritance *now?*
(166)

13. What is Bruce''s paraphrase of Jeremiah 29:11-13?
(166-167)

14. Paraphrase John 16:13.

15. **Review**: In I John 4:17b, what is the one word we have read incorrectly?

16. Discuss Bruce''s visit with Natalia.
(168-170)

17. Discuss the Chariot Rides.
(170-172)

18. Do you need to get out of a box? Are you holding some traditions of men as "gospel?" Are some beliefs/unbeliefs keeping you in bondage?
48

Chapter Eight
Translation by Faith: Going

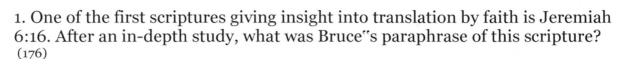

1. One of the first scriptures giving insight into translation by faith is Jeremiah 6:16. After an in-depth study, what was Bruce''s paraphrase of this scripture? (176)

2. What does "old paths" mean?

3. How do we find and walk in these ancient paths? (176-177)

4. What is a good prayer to pray concerning ancient paths?

5. Discuss Bruce's first experience with translation on a trip from Edmonds, WA to Spokane, WA.

6. **Exercise:** Apply your faith this week to be translated on a routine trip from one place to another. Be willing for the Lord to do whatever He chooses.

7. What were the three keys on a ring (from a previous visitation)? (178-179)

8. What is the purpose of the keys? (179)

9. How does one use a spiritual key? (179)

10. **Review:** Why did Uzziah have to die before the Lord could be seen? (179-181)
49

11. The crucified life, sanctification, death to fleshly carnal desires... What is the result of paying this price? (181)

12. **Review:** What are some first works of Jesus that we would rather skip over so we can just do the miracles?
(181-182)

13. Jesus grew up in Nazareth. What is the literal meaning of Nazareth?
(181)

14. The seraphim are crying, "Holy! Holy! Holy! Is the Lord of hosts." (Isaiah 6:3) What is a better translation of Holy, Holy, Holy?
(183)

15. How did people hear from God at Shiloh and how does this apply to us?
(183-184)

16. Early Celtic Christians in Ireland and Wales had an understanding that places like Shiloh were called a _____ place where the veil between this reality and that reality was so thin through prayer, sanctification and through intercession and worship that Heaven was literally within reach. It was easy to "connect" with the spirit realm because of the atmosphere that had been created.
(183-184)

17. What is a good prayer to pray concerning a thin place?

18. Look at the progression in Isaiah 6. First, Pride dies, then there is a revelation of his true spiritual condition, and as Isaiah understood his spiritual condition, lastly, there is a transaction that takes place as God atones, cleanses, and does away with those things that have hindered us from entering into the fullness of His promise. What is the application for us?

19. How do we begin to walk and interact with heaven?
(183-184)

20. In Genesis 24:1-61, finding a bride for Isaac, Abraham is a type of the Father, and the servant (Eleazer) is a type of the Holy Spirit. "Eleazer" means "comforter or _____."

21.   One of the keys of this story is the _____ heart that rules over all the Father has. The bondservant is released to steward all the Father has, not just part of His possessions.
(191-192)

22. *Yalak*, translated go and follow me, means journey and _____.
(187,192)

23. It was necessary for Rebecca to _____ and go to Isaac.

(192)

24. When God tested Abraham telling him to sacrifice Isaac, how old was Isaac? When was Isaac seen again, after Abraham offered him as a sacrifice on Mount Moriah?

25. Rebecca"s test was to water the camels. How much water does a thirsty camel drink? This certainly demonstrates a servant"s heart in Rebecca!
(195)

26. Discuss Bruce"s translation to Sydney, Australia. What was he doing when he felt himself being sucked out of his body?
(199-201)

27. You make the choice, and He will make the _____! You become willing, and He will be your _____!
(202)

Chapter Nine
The Glory Within

1. Romans 13:14 says, *But put ye on the Lord Jesus Christ and make no provision for the flesh to fulfill the lusts thereof.* The word "put on" is the Greek word *endueo* and is the same Greek word used when it says that the Holy Spirit will come upon you and you will be endued (*endueo*) with power from on high. It means "to be _____ in the sense of sinking into a garment".
 (205-206)

2. The word picture for *endueo* is
_____.
(205-206)

3. Another significant word in Romans 13:14 is "provision." When we put on Jesus, we make no provision for the flesh. "Provision" means you are not going to have any _____ nor plan in advance for the things of the flesh.
 (206)

4. **Review:** We have read the scriptures in past tense instead of present tense. 1 John 4:17 says this, *Herein is our love made perfect that we may have boldness in
the day of judgment because even as He _____, so are we in this world.* Most of our lives as believers we have been trying to live as He *was*. While that has merit and is a good foundation and starting point, we need to look at what Jesus is like right now and what He is doing right now. In that way, we can move toward the potential of this promise of being as He *is* in this world.
(207)

5. The Bible has everything we need for life and godliness. It has every promise we need, but if we don"t _____ what has been so freely given us, we will never walk in it.
 (207)

6. A _____ assent is not an acceptance of a _____.
 (207)

7. How do we examine ourselves so we know that we are not just mentally agreeing with the Word of God?
(207)

8. What is the first example of a "work" we can do, given in the book? What is the second example?
(208)

9. **Review:** Can a man be in two places at one time? Explain.
(208)

10. Fulfilling our destiny with our own strength leads to the_____.
(210)

11. Exodus 3:1-5 says, *Now, Moses kept the flock of Jethro, his father-in-law, the Priest of Midian, and he led the flock to the back side of the desert and came to the mountain of God, even to Horeb.* What does Mount Horeb mean?
(210)

12. How did Moses endure the wilderness?
(210)

13. Do we need to change our paradigm about how we think about and want to avoid the wilderness?
(210)

14. Why did Paul glory in trials?
(211)

5. The more anointing you have without brokenness, the greater the _____ is in the making.
(212)

16. Brokenness leads to _____.
(212)

17. Based on his advice to the young people Bruce took to Fiji concerning how they prayed about the trip, examine your own prayers and hold them up against this example and Bruce"s example of determining God"s will in a matter.
(212-213)

18. Explain how we are living in the seventh day now and what God speaking to Moses out of the cloud on the seventh day means to us.
(213-215)

19. Discuss Moses'' experience with the Glory and the processes of death, decay, and corruption slowing down.
(215)

20. You will fulfill your destiny if you are _____ to the Lord.
(215)

21. When the Glory came, Moses talked to the Lord _____.
(216)

22. When the Glory of God comes into contact with anything that is not immortal, it _____ the natural law of death and decay.
(216-217)

23. We have limited God with our _____.
(217)

24. The word, "*shekinah*," as in *Shekinah* Glory, means "resting or _____."
(217)

25. Why are we praying wrong when we ask the Lord to send His Glory?

Dr. Bruce D. Allen

Chapter Ten
The Glory Released

1. When the Lord instructed Bruce to release the Glory concerning the mosquitoes, how did he pray?
(221-222)

2. Isaiah 4:5 says, *The Lord will create above every dwelling place of Mount Zion and upon her assemblies, a cloud and smoke by day and the shining of a flaming fire by night. For over all the glory shall be a covering.* "Covering" means
_____ or _____.
(221-222)

3. Corporately, you are _____ _____. Individually, you are dwelling _____. The Lord said he would create above all of us a canopy of Glory.
(222)

4. **Application:** Release the canopy of Glory:
  a) over your marriage
b) over your workplace
c) over your children and siblings
d) over disease
e) over _____

5. In Isaiah 4:5, "smoke" means "the _____ or anger of Yahweh."
(222)

6. In Isaiah 4:5, "flaming fire" means "sharply polished _____."
God is going to put the terror of Yahweh on my enemies.
(223)

7. In Isaiah 4:5, the word "covering" (NKJV), also translated as "defense" in the KJV, is the Hebrew word *huppa,* which means "a covering; to cover, to veil, to _____ and protect.
(223)

8. What are we protected from by the *huppa* of God"s Glory?
(224)

9. Give some examples of Jesus walking in the canopy of God"s Glory.
(224)

10. The word "shadow" in Isaiah 4:6 *(there shall be a tabernacle for a shadow in the day of heat)* and in Psalm 91:1 *(He who dwells in the secret place of the Most Highshall abide under the shadow of the almighty)* are the same word and means

_____.

(224)

11. Give some examples of how walking in the canopy of God"s Glory should affect you and me?
(224-226)

12. If healing is the children"s bread, what belongs to a mature son?
(226)

13. So how do we get from where we have walked in the past to where we should be?
(226)

14. Discuss Bruce"s example of mosquitoes in Fiji, while visiting Reshma"s family. How would you apply this to yourself?
(226-227)

15. Discuss the example of Bruce"s needed dental work and his toothache. How would you apply this to yourself?
(228-229)

58
Study Guide
16. The first response we should have in every situation is to "_____ _____."
(228)

17. Discuss the mosquitoes at the family barbeque. How would you apply this to a family situation?
(228-229)

1
8. What other pests does the Glory eliminate?
(229)

19. Discuss the canopy of God''s Glory and the minister in Africa.
(229-230)

20. What is the curse from which Christ redeemed us? (Galatians 3:13)
(230)

21. There were many miracles in Acts after the disciples were *endueod* with power. Acts 5 brings a shift as Peter''s shadow healed people. "Shadow" does not mean shadow as we think of it. Shadow means "an effluence and a
_____" that came forth out of Peter from within, and anybody that came in the presence of that radiance was healed.
(231)

22. The word "overshadow" used in the KJV literally means "to
_____
in a haze of brilliancy." Charles Finney walked in this without realizing what it was. He would go through town on a train and there was such an effluence, a radiance of the Glory that was upon him that people would begin to drop and cry out for salvation.
(231)

23. **Meditate on this**: The Glory that was in Jesus began to so radiate from out of
Him, so that it even affected His clothing and His countenance. Not only that, it eliminated the barrier between the natural realm and the spiritual, so that He was able to talk face to face with Moses and Elijah!
(232)

24. **Exercise:** Meditate on the fact that you are in the Glory and the Glory is in you.
(232-233)

25. **Exercise:** Begin to practice releasing what is in you. Release it! Release it! Then practice all the time! Shortly you will begin to have supernatural faceto-face Encounters with the King of Glory, Jesus! Release the Glory when you go to the Post Office. When you go to the Restaurant, release the Glory. When you get on an airplane, release the Glory. Let God demonstrate his ways around you.
(233)

26. Psalms 84:11 - *For the LORD God is a sun and shield; The LORD will give grace and glory; No good thing will He withhold from those who walk uprightly.* The word "sun" is the Hebrew word *shemesh* which means "a _____ battlement." This represents a protected place carved out for us.
(234)

27. Discuss the experience of the Muslim village.
(234-235)

28. What is a good paraphrase of Isaiah 4:5-6?
(235)

29. Discuss demons manifesting in Ireland.
(235-236)

30. Discuss the dream of Bruce"s friend.
(237)

31. Give an instance in the Old Testament or in the New Testament that gives an example of encounters with God or Jesus.
(241)

32. Pray the prayer on page 238.
60

Gazing into Glory Study Guide Answers
Bruce D. Allen
Study Guide Answers *Gazing into Glory*

Prayer

Father, thank you for the work of Bruce Allen. Answer his prayer that I enter into my birthright to see into the realm of the Spirit and to be activated to walk in that realm regularly.

Preface

1. Answers will vary for demonstrating personal hunger.

2. Answers will vary for demonstrating many ways man"s traditions have replaced the Word. One example is: a person cannot pray for another until graduating from seminary.

3. unbelief

4. discernment, Word

5. yes, yes.
Repentance prayer follows.
Prayer
Father, forgive me for my ignorance of Your ways, for the fear I"ve allowed in my life, and for the unbelief I"ve walked in. I repent and turn away from these sins.

6. Discernment is not judgment based upon our belief system, regardless of what scripture teaches In the CD Album *Gazing into Glory*, Bruce commented that one way to develop discernment is by spending all our time on truth and not focusing on error.

(TheCDs are available on the website: stillwatersinternationalministries.com)

7. John 14:12 - *Most assuredly, I say to you, he who believes in Me, the works that I do he will do also; and greater works than these he will do, because I go to My Father.*
a) We will do the works that Jesus does
b) We will do greater works than Jesus does

8. Hebrews 5:7-8 –
Who, in the days of His flesh, when He had offered up prayers and supplications, with vehement cries and tears to Him who was able to save Him from death, and was heard because of His godly fear, though He was a Son, yet He learned obedience by the things which He suffered.
  Select two:
a) prayer and supplications with strong crying and tears
b) godly fear
c) obedience through suffering

9. character

10. Philippians 2:5-8 –
5
64
8
Let this mind be in you which was also in Christ Jesus, who, being in the form of God, did not consider it robbery to be equal with God, but made Himself of no reputation, taking the form of a bondservant, and coming in the likeness of men. And being found in appearance as a man, He humbled Himself and became obedient to the point of death, even the death of the cross.
8
Select two:
a) have the mind of Christ
b) become a servant
c) humble ourselves
d) become obedient unto death.

11. bondservant

7
6
12. purge
Prayer follows.
Study Guide Answers
Prayer
Father, let the Holy Spirit purge me of _____.

Forgive me for pride, self-centeredness, and practicing a form of godliness without Your power. Purge me from dead works and the lust of my carnal nature.

13. personal answer and personal prayer

14. power of God

15. Prayer follows.

Prayer
When I am around people who are ignorant of You, Father, let your power be demonstrated through me.

16. 1) word of wisdom
2) word of knowledge
3) discerning of spirits
4) faith
5) healing
6) working of miracles
7) prophecy
8) tongues
9) the interpretation of tongues

17. Mark 16:17-18 –
And these signs shall follow them that believe; In my name shall they cast out devils; they shall speak with new tongues; They shall take up serpents; and if they drink any deadly thing, it shall not hurt them; they shall lay hands on the sick, and they shall recover.
a) cast out devils
b) speak with new tongues
c) take up serpents
d) if they drink any deadly thing, it shall not hurt them
e) lay hands on the sick, and they shall recover.
65
18. grow in Christ and bear greater fruit for the kingdom

19. Prayer follows.
Prayer
Make me grow in Christ, and make me bear greater fruit for the kingdom.

20. personal answer

Introduction

1. The Greco-Roman mindset means that we have to figure out how God can do something before we actually believe that He can do it.

2. The Jewish people understood that the Lord is a supernatural Being and is above natural law; nothing is impossible with Him. They understood that an omnipotent God could not be understood with a finite mind so they lived with an understanding of the supernatural, which was beyond their ability to reason.

3. God said it, and that"s good enough for me; I don"t have to understand it. In the *Gazing into Glory* CD Album, Bruce commented: "You said it; I believe it. Will you explain it to me?" He also said, "Don"t try to figure God out. Just agree with him."

4. Luke 24:45 - *And He opened their understanding, that they might comprehend the*
scriptures.

5. Prayer follows.
Prayer
Open my understanding that I may comprehend the scriptures more.

6. Luke 8:10 - *And He said, To you it has been given to know the mysteries of the kingdom*
of God, but to the rest it is given in parables, that „Seeing they may not see, And hearing they may not understand.'

7. Prayer follows.
Prayer
Grant to me that I may know the mysteries of the kingdom more.
Open my eyes that I may see more and my ears that I may hear more.
68

Chapter One Answers
Seeing: A Supernaturally Natural Occurrence

2. Following is the prayer.

3. False!

Prayer
Father, activate my spiritual eyesight.

4. Because God gave everyone physical sight so that they could see. Likewise God gives spiritual eyesight to all of His children so that they can see.

5. unscriptural

6. The answer, scripturally, is yes. You are on this earth, and the Bible says you are seated together with him in heavenly places.
Ephesians 2:6 - *and raised us up together, and made us sit together in the heavenly places in Christ Jesus...*

7. personal exercise

We have settled for what we see with our physical eyes. Bruce''s quantum physicist friend, David Van Koevering, points out in conferences that the physical realm, compared to the invisible realm, is like comparing 2 inches (physical) to 50 miles (invisible).
In the CD Album *Gazing into Glory*, Bruce said that our destiny far surpasses anything we can imagine it to be.

8. We limit God by creating a supernatural God in our own image based on our own understanding.

9. c) both practicing and trial and error!

10. Salvation is the entry point or portal. Once you have accepted Christ you then have free access into a realm of existence you never knew before. Salvation unlocks the door.

11. Many scriptures. This is an open-ended discussion.

12. inheritance

13. d) all of the above

14. b) all of God''s children

15. c) both of the above
Matthew 28:18-19 -
*And Jesus came and spoke to them, saying, "All authority has
been given to Me in heaven and on earth. Go therefore and make disciples of all
the nations, baptizing them in the name of the Father and of the Son and of the
Holy Spirit,*
70
19 Psalm 8:6 - *You have made him to have dominion over the works of Your
hands; You have put all things under his feet,*

16. c) both of the above

17. busyness, distractions, "instant" mindset without patience to wait on God, etc.

18. c) both of the above

19. The law of first mention refers to the first time something is mentioned in the
Bible. From that point on you can use this first mention as a base point to
interpret all other scriptures speaking of the same subject. An example of first
mention can be found in Genesis 1:26-31, which tells us that man was created
on the sixth day. From that point on we realize that six is the number of man.
Anytime you read the word "man" in scripture or see the number six, you
know He is talking about flesh, or man.

20. face-to-face

21. Yes, our relationship with God changed with the fall...until Jesus came. Today
our relationship with God has been restored because Jesus, the second Adam,
was crucified on the cross and shed His blood that we may once again enter
into relationship with the Father. We have now been reinstated to that place of
relationship with God, without the need for a veil, without the posturing,
without the snare of religious traditions.

22. Exercise setting your heart and mind on Christ when you go to bed.

23. f) All of the above

24. The answers will vary as you, by the Blood of Jesus, create an "atmosphere" because you are the temple of the Holy Spirit. The principle from the law of first mention in the story of Jacob is that the house of God is the gateway of heaven (Genesis 28:17), and we are the house of God (I Corinthians 6:19).

25. Prayer follows.

Prayer
Father, grant me a face-to-face relationship with You.

26. see, hear

27. g) All of the above

28. True
From the CD Album *Gazing into Glory,* Bruce comments: "He speaks in dreams, visions, face to face encounters, impressions, His word, anointed preaching, music. HE SPEAKS. We miss it because we try to develop faith in our ability to hear. Stop it. Put you faith where it belongs. Have faith in God to speak loud enough that you can"t help but hear."

29. released

30. spoke

31. Negative thoughts are not sin, until you start focusing on them and meditating on them. Then they drop into your heart where sin is conceived.

32. see

33. no

34. The continual present tense means, "what is happening now." What Jesus is doing right now, I can do also.

35. personal answer
One aspect of this is that Jesus is now stepping through the veil from one dimension to another.

36. Passion is pursuit. It is not just thinking about something, but pursuing it. Zacchaeus put aside his dignity as a chief tax collector and climbed a sycamore tree in his pursuit of Jesus. Passion causes us to do something outside the norm and outside cultural decorum. Passion can be seen by spending time in the Word, spending hours praying, spending days fasting, etc.

37. purity

72
38. see

39. revelation

40. Bartimaeus throwing his cloak off meant he was severing all affiliation with his previous life. His cloak was his "license" to beg so he had made a commitment to not turn back.

41. personal answer

42. "Blind" means "to envelop with smoke; to inflate with self-conceit; high-minded, be lifted up with pride, be proud."

43. d) All of the above

44. obedience

45. "Manifest" means to "cause to be seen; to openly show." *(The Complete Word Study Dictionary)*. Jesus will openly show Himself to those who love Him and who keep His commandments.

46. Prayer follows.
Prayer
Lord, I want to be obedient to this Word as best I can.
Help me in my lack of obedience.

47. d) All of the above

Bruce states in conferences that the Christian life is a progression of breaking out of man-made boxes.

48. b) character, honor, authority

Many times we practice correct religious protocol of including "in Jesus" name" in our prayers, without making sure our own character is the character of Jesus.

49. Paraphrase of John 14:13:
Whatever you ask the Father, with Christ-like character, He will do it.

50. Paraphrase of Matthew 18:20:
Where two or three are gathered in my character, I am there in the midst of them.

51. Prayer follows.

Prayer
God, whatever you want, I want!

Chapter Two Answers
Seeing: A Face-to-Face Reality

1. Will you allow Jesus to reveal Himself as He truly is and to do in your life what He desires to do?

2. John 8:38 should be enough to challenge us to move forward into the possibility and promise of "seeing" and "doing."

3. We will SEE heaven open and we will SEE angels. From that point forward, the moment Jesus spoke those words, He indicated that as His followers we will see the angels of God ascending and descending. We are the body of Christ (1 Corinthians 12:27).

4. We have overlooked the insight that this scripture doesn"t say Jesus will return "at the second coming." There are millions of people having face-to-face encounters with the living Jesus in this hour. From resurrection morning until the ascension at Bethel 40 days later, Jesus appeared to 90% of the then known church in a resurrected body. We find in 1 Corinthians 15:5-6 that Jesus was seen by the twelve and then upwards of five hundred witnesses at one time. In the same way He left, He is coming again, appearing to many individuals and even to regions not yet evangelized.

5. We have overlooked the understanding that Uzziah represented pride. We cannot see the Lord as long as pride rules us. King Uzziah was crowned King at the age of 16 (2 Chronicles 26:1), and he did what was right in the sight of the Lord. As long as he did so, God made him prosper (v 5). However pride entered his heart, and he offered incense to the Lord rather than allowing the Priesthood to do so. Because of this pride he was struck with leprosy and remained in that condition until the day he died. Isaiah 6:1 could be re-written as, *In the year that pride died, I saw the Lord.*
6. a) pride

7. True

8. Uzziah failed the test of prosperity and abundant blessings because of pride in his own abilities.

9. doctrines

10. The selfishness and "give me" attitude of the immature prodigal son is like the church today. As the prodigal wasted his inheritance, so we cannot squander our gifts only in the church. We must sow into the *harvest field*. Maturity comes in recognizing the gift and asking, "make me" instead of "give me." The purpose of our life is not exclusively to be focused upon the "doing," but rather upon the "becoming." To become like Jesus is the major pursuit of our life.

11. Give away the anointing and revelation you have to others.

12. money

13. d) All of the above

14. make me

15. personal answer
In a conference, Bruce said we should pray for our loved ones by asking that they have a revelation from God. He instructed us to stop looking at the circumstances.
Prayer follows.
Prayer

Give _____ (name of person) a revelation that "make me" (more like Christ) is more important than "give me" (my selfish desires).
76

16. maturity
17. a) becoming like Jesus and b) worshipping by obedience.

18. We are to focus on the things that are not seen.
2 Corinthians 4:17-18 –
For our light affliction, which is but for a moment working
for us, is a far more exceeding and eternal weight of glory.
17
While we do not look at
the things which are seen, but at the things which are not seen. For the things
which are seen are temporary, but the things which are not seen are eternal.
77
18

19. We see the invisible things that are not seen by our encounters with the Lord. In order to perceive and walk in an open heaven, we must be able to develop a visual capacity. Until we come to the place to see the invisible, we use the tool

of our sanctified imagination.

20. Spiritual blindness is more incapacitating than physical blindness because the realm of the spirit, not the physical realm, is the true reality. Our physical world is a foreshadow of the spiritual realm. We have over-exercised our natural senses and have become dependant on them. Thus we have become spiritually handicapped. Editor's Note: This study is spiritual therapy/ exercise to help us overcome our spiritual handicap.

21. We also connect spiritually by touch, taste, smell, and hearing.

22. personal experience
In the CD Album *Gazing into Glory*, Bruce commented that we have more than five senses. We also have the sense of "go."

23. The word "see" literally means "see." The Greek word is *eido* (Strong's #1492) and means to see literally or figuratively. So for each of us, it means, if we are born again, we can see the kingdom of God, period!

24. In scripture, seven is the number of "rest, covenant promise fulfilled and completion." Eight signifies "new beginnings." Seven and one-half, being halfway between seven and eight, speaks of a transition from one day or season into another.

25. morning
(Recommended reading: *Promise of the Third Day* by Bruce Allen)

26. True

27. consistent passion

28. From the time of Jesus until the turn of the century we have completed two thousand years, or two days. Historically we can also count backward four thousand years to Adam. So from Adam until the turn of the century we have completed six thousand years or, according to this scripture, six days. We are now early in the morning on the seventh day.
(Recommended reading: *Prophetic Promise of the Seventh Day*)

29. On the seventh day, Jesus revealed the kingdom of God to Peter, James and John in a way they had never experienced before. They saw an aspect of the kingdom in a way they had never conceived of because with their eyes wide

open they saw through the veil of time into eternity and witnessed Jesus speaking to Moses and Elijah face-to-face! We are prophetically in the 7 day.

30. We should separate ourselves more often and pray in a quiet place alone.
78

31. Hebrew oral tradition regarding Jesus and His prayer time was that He would separate Himself from the press of people and go off into a mountain to be with the Lord. He would sit down and begin to dialogue with His Father by telling Him what He did that day. He would review His day with the Lord. When He was done, the Father would tell Him and show Him what he would see and do the next day so Jesus would know where He would go, who He would meet, and what exactly was going to happen. In John 5:19 He only does what He sees the Father doing.

32. Possible answers:
Jeremiah 33:3 - *Call to Me, and I will answer you, and show you great and might things, which you do not know.*
John 16:13 - *The Holy Spirit will lead us and guide us into all truth and will show us things to come.*

33. As a new creation in Christ we now have access to the Father. All things have become new.
2 Corinthians 5:17 - *Therefore, if anyone is in Christ, he is a new creation; old things have passed away; behold, all things have become new.*

34. In 1 Timothy 6:16, the word "man" is the Greek word *anthropos* and means "sinful man." In other words, it is sinful man who has never seen, nor ever can see, the Lord who dwells in unapproachable light. We the redeemed are already seated in heavenly places with him. (Ephesians 2:6)

35. Possible answers:

Isaiah 6:1 - *In the year that king Uzziah died I saw the Lord.*
Genesis 32:30 - *And Jacob called the name of the place Peniel: for „I have seen God face-to-face, and my life is preserved.*
Exodus 24:9-11 -
Then Moses went up, also Aaron, Nadab, and Abihu, and seventy of the elders of Israel,
9
and they saw the God of Israel. And there was under His feet as

it were a paved work of sapphire stone, and it was like the very heavens in its clarity.
11
10
But on the nobles of the children of Israel He did not lay His hand. So they saw God, and they ate and drank.
 Exodus 33:11 – *And the Lord spake unto Moses face to face, as a man speaketh unto his*
friend...
79
36. face-to-face!

37. We humans, in the spirit realm, are beings of overwhelming light.

38. Unconfessed sin and blending in with the world (compromise) rather than standing out as a shining example. That is why it is so vitally important to be quick to repent and apply the blood of Jesus.

39. Discussion of vision on the airplane
 Christians were wearing drab clothes instead of the white garments that came with the new birth. Unconfessed sin, cares of this world, and compromise dulled the clothes.

40. sanctify

41. Just as Adam did, we are quick to point the finger in every direction but ourselves when in truth, the easiest way to victory is simply saying, "Father, forgive me."

42. No, Jesus is not going against scripture. The answer lies in our understanding of
what it means to be "dead."
 Deuteronomy 18:10-12 - *There shall not be found among you anyone who makes his son or his daughter pass through the fire, or one who practices witchcraft, or a soothsayer, or one who interprets omens, or a sorcerer, or one who conjures spells,*
or a medium, or a spiritist, or one who calls up the dead. For all who do such things are an abomination to the Lord.

43. In the New Testament there is a distinction between those who have accepted Christ and are now *alive* in Him and those who are without Christ and *dead* in their trespasses and sins. Jesus was not communicating with the dead. He was

communicating with those who were part of the family of God already in Glory. Also in the New Testament, whenever a redeemed individual or a child was "dead" according to the understanding of the world, they were said to be "asleep" by Jesus or the apostles.

Ephesians. 2:1 - *And you He made alive, who were dead in trespasses and sins.*

Colossians. 2:13 - *And you, being dead in your trespasses and the uncircumcision of*

your flesh, He has made alive together with Him, having forgiven you all trespasses.

44. Instant knowledge comes when there is interaction with the Spirit, as part of the
pattern of visitation, revelation, and activation.

45. All of the above

46. We have seen multitudes of people going down under the power and anointing of God, showing us that when a natural man comes into contact with the supernatural power of God, the human body simply short-circuits. There must come a time, however, when we are strengthened to the point where we can stand under a greater weight of glory. If the Glory of God is going to cover the earth like the waters cover the seas, and our response to that glory is to continually be slain in the spirit, does that mean everybody is going to be dropping all over the earth? We are going to be strengthened in the glory to the point where we can stand in the very atmosphere of heaven.

47. The Glory of God is the atmosphere of heaven.

48. "See" means "see!" Don''t change it and make it mystical. Don''t give it other definitions. Your birthright is to see clearly into the spirit realm and to know Him face-to-face.

49. We don''t worship angels, we don''t command angels, and we don''t ask God to show us angels!

50. Sometimes an angel is standing around looking bored when that particular church is not accomplishing nor fulfilling its destiny. Other times angels that look like they''re worn out. Their swords are drawn, and they look as if they''ve been sweating. The church in this case has been effective in their commission and vision from the Lord. The angel looks wearied because he has been either warding off the attacks of the enemy and/or being sent forth to accomplish the

Father"s will through the intercessions, prayers and decrees of the group of believers in that house.

51. False. It is our birthright and our inheritance to *see* the kingdom of God! Even children receive visions and see angels.

52. d) today
Today is all we have so we should live each day with the expectation of Jesus" return... today!

53. language

54. personal answer
 Prayer follows.
Prayer
Father, begin to stir in my heart and the hearts of _____ so that we long to know you face-to-face. Your Word states that if we ask you for a fish you will not give us a rock, so right now I ask that you activate this revelation within me and within _____. Open our eyes to see.
82

Chapter Three Answers
The Sanctified Imagination: Eyes on Him

1. Our focus is on the Spiritual realm, on heavenly places, and on being seated with Him in heavenly places (Ephesians 2:6), no matter where we are on this earth or what is going on around us! (Other answers apply.)

2. Our imagination is our reality, according to Jesus!

3. Thoughts are not the problem: engaging those thoughts and meditating on them will cause them to drop into our heart where they become sinful attitudes which lead to sinful behavior.

4. our mind

5. captive

6. When recognizing my thoughts are not of God, I immediately stop thinking those thoughts and deliberately change to meditating on/memorizing scripture or imagining sanctified thoughts.
 2 Corinthians 10:5 - *casting down arguments and every high thing that exalts itselfagainst the knowledge of God, bringing every thought into captivity to the obedience of Christ.*

7. Paul is not just talking about ordinary understanding and knowledge. Understanding and knowledge in this scripture have "eyes" and include how we look and think about things.

8. *dianoya* and *dialogisimo*

9. imagination; Matthew 22:37 contains *dianoya*.
 Matthew 22:37 - *Jesus said unto him "You shall love the Lord your God with all your heart, your soul, and your mind (dianoya). This is the first commandment with promise."*

10. Paraphrase of Matthew 22:37 – You shall love the Lord your God with all your heart, your soul, and your imagination. This is the first commandment with promise.

11. We love the Lord with our imagination the same way we love a person with our imagination. When we are in love with someone, it is natural to continually or constantly "see" that person in your imagination. You think about what they looked like at that special moment when the light hit them just so, and you think about the look of joy or sorrow on their face during that certain moment etc. Perhaps you imagine your next encounter with the one you love. When we learn to keep the Lord constantly at the forefront of our thoughts, we in turn "see" Him in our minds" eye and as such we are fulfilling scripture.

12. personal exercise
Use the examples listed in the book or your own example of a location, picturing yourself in the location, in your imagination. Which of your five senses (seeing, hearing, touching, smelling, tasting) were involved? Did your soul (emotions) get involved? Did you feel happy or sad or comforted? Did you "see" a scene take on a life of its own?

13. The devil never created anything. He only twists the truth and counterfeits Gods. We must remember God instructed us to love Him with our (Greek word) *dianoya*.
In the *Gazing into Glory* CD Album, Bruce commented: The devil has not created anything except sin. He steals everything from God and perverts it; then we call it New Age. There is nothing new about it!

14. *The New Dictionary of Theology*, Volume 3 says when the Greek word *dianoya* is used in relation to the heart, it always means "imagination."

15. *Vine"s* dictionary says *dianoya* is a faculty renewed by the Holy Spirit and called imagination. Our imagination must be renewed or sanctified by the Holy Spirit; then it will become a useful weapon in our arsenal.

16. personal answer
 Obey God!

17. reckon thoroughly
 Luke 1:29 speaks about Mary meeting Gabriel.
 Luke 1:29 - *And when she saw him, she was troubled at his saying, and cast in* (her logical, reasoning) *mind what manner of salutation this should be.*

18. A wandering mind hinders our growth! As followers of Christ, we need to *cast*

down any thought or imagination that would exalt itself against the knowledge of God, and take every thought captive to the obedience of Christ (2 Corinthians 10:5). When we do not do so, we hamper and hinder ourselves in our spiritual growth. The majority of Christians allow their mind to wander anywhere it wants at any time.

19. sanctify

20. Understanding and using the gift of your imagination has the potential to release you to level of awareness that leaves very little room for the enemy. His time worn schemes will no longer be effective in your life.

21. Discussion of a person who, after receiving prayer for healing, still "saw herself" being sick and going to the doctor. We apply this to ourselves by "seeing" ourselves as healed after receiving prayer.

22. There is a connection between the part of your mind that controls images, pictures, dreams and the heart. The heart makes contact with the spirit realm, and the mouth releases the power of that realm. Another way to say this is that the imagination makes contact with the spirit realm, and out of the abundance of the heart, you speak agreement or disagreement with what the Spirit or Word says by what you are "seeing" in your imagination.

23. Prayers for healing, seeing correctly the healing in oneself

24. b) *dialogisimo* or strong logical mind
 c) a Greek mindset or needing to understand how God can do some-thing before believing He can do it

25. imagination

26. photograph

27. The eyes of our understanding are enlightened; the eyes of our understanding are *fotitsmo*. The eyes of our understanding are looking at a photograph. With the eyes of our understanding, we see photographs or snapshots of heaven.

28. 1) sanctifies his imagination by thinking on right things, heavenly things, spiritual things, etc and 2) frames pictures of these heavenly things, of the Kingdom of God *in* his imagination. As we follow this example, something supernatural will begin to occur.

29. connect; activation

30. "Activation" means as you practice framing your own pictures, you will move from framing your pictures to actually seeing into the realm of the spirit with your eyes wide open. What you see in your imagination actually takes on life apart from your imagination.
86
Study Guide Answers
31.   2 Corinthians 3:18 - We are changed into the same image from glory to glory.

32. "That eyes of your imagination might receive pictures of the Kingdom of Heaven, so that you might know your destiny."

33. your paraphrase
An example: The eyes of my imagination receive pictures of the kingdom of heaven, and I know my assignment.

34. a sanctified imagination
Remember that Jesus considered imagination to be reality. (Matthew 5:28/p 85)

35. We begin to learn a new "language" that becomes uniquely our language with God. Visions are a language; a picture paints a thousand words. The more we apply this principle, the more fluent we become, and the more fluent we become, the quicker the activation.

36. True

37. The meaning of *haga* is "murmur; to ponder, *imagine*, meditate, mutter or roar."

38. Joshua 1:8 tells us to meditate on, mutter with our voice, properly frame pictures and imagine scripture all of the time! Meditation brings success.
 Joshua 1:8 - *This book of the law shall not depart out of your mouth, but you shall*
meditate (ponder and imagine) *therein day and night, that you may observe to do according to all that is written therein. For then you shall make your way prosperous, and then you shall have good success.*

39. Meditate in the Greek is *dianoya*, which means to imagine or frame pictures in your imagination (in 1 Timothy 4:15)

40. 1 Timothy 1:14-15 paraphrase - Neglect not the gift that is in you, which was given you by prophecy, with the laying on of the hands of the presbytery. Imagine properly framed pictures of these things, give yourself wholly to them; that your profiting may appear to all.

41. True

42. Exercise involving the healing of the leper

43. Discussion of Bruce overcoming shyness

44. God''s people are destroyed for lack of knowledge.
 Hosea 4:6 - *My people are destroyed for lack of knowledge.*

45. imagined

46. yes

47. Matthew 18:19 - *Again I say to you that if two of you agree on earth concerning anything that they ask, it will be done for them by My Father in heaven.*

48. to be aware, behold, look on

49. John 16:13 – *However, when He, the Spirit of truth, has come, He will guide you into all truth; for He will not speak on His own authority, but whatever He hears He will speak; and He will tell you things to come.*
John on the Isle of Patmos saw things to come.
Daniel saw things to come

50. seeing
88
Study Guide Answers
51. Two keys to seeing the invisible are 1) a consuming passion for Him and 2) building a bridge between the natural and the supernatural with a sanctified imagination.

52. mind or the thing framed in your imagination

53. Paraphrase for Isaiah 26:3 — You will keep him in perfect peace, whose imagination properly forms images of You which reflects trust in You.

54. Hebrews 12:2 - *Looking unto Jesus, the author and finisher of your faith.*
Colossians 3:2 - *Set your affection on things above, not on things on the earth.*
James 4:8 - *Draw near to God and he will draw near to you.*

55. d) All of the above.

56. religion

In the *Gazing into Glory* CD Album, Bruce commented that the Christian life is a progression of breaking out of man-made boxes.

57. An unsanctified imagination is thinking or meditating on worldly things, thinking or meditating totally with your logical mind, or thinking or meditating on unpleasant situations or people, worrying about the cares of this world, etc. Philippians 4:8 provides guidelines for sanctifying our mind.
Philippians 4:8 - *Finally, brethren, whatsoever things are true, whatsoever things are honest, whatsoever things are just, whatsoever things are pure, whatsoever things are lovely, whatsoever things are of good report; if there be any virtue, and if there be any praise, think on these things.*

Chapter Four Answers
The Sanctified Imagination: Activating Adventure

1. True

2. Discussion of man meeting with Jesus, properly framing pictures of Him. This is a perfect example of connecting with what we focus on and activating what we connect with.

3. Exercise of visualizing Jesus. Bruce purposefully focuses on heavenly things ten minutes each day as a discipline.

4. False
Most of us can only focus on one thing for eight to ten seconds!

5. f) All of the above

6. sanctified imagination

7. The baptism of the Holy Spirit brought the scriptures to life for Bruce. Ask the Lord for this gift and/or ask someone who has received this experience to lay hands on you and pray for you to receive it.

8. He recognized the devil was trying to steal Bible reading from him so he

resisted the pull to sleep instead of read, and told the devil he was going to read another chapter if sleep tried to come on him.

9. Discussion. (Bruce had a passion for more of God and knew that God is no respecter of person. What He does for one, He will do for another.)

10. revisit

11. Bruce framed the picture of Jesus as an everyday discipline of at least ten minutes per day minimum. Your commitment?

12. Exercise

13. Test **every** spirit **every** time! No matter who or what it looks like, even if it appears to be Jesus, test every spirit every time.

14. You and I are like radio tuners. We are tuned in to this natural realm because we set our "frequency" to interact with this realm. As the redeemed however, we have the ability to "tune in" to a much higher frequency of the spirit realm. We choose our frequency. We can continue operating in the lower spectrum, the natural realm, or we can learn to fine tune our "receiver" and connect with the frequency of the spirit realm. *Gazing into Glory* will help you fine tune your receiver The angels hearken to the voice of God, not to the voice of man. As we pray in our heavenly language, it is the Spirit praying through us, not we ourselves. In doing this, the Lord sends His messengers to accomplish His word, not our word.

15. angels

16. imaginations

92
Study Guide Answers

17. When we don''t sanctify our thought life, and those thoughts are contrary to the Word of God and the Heart of God, they are wicked imaginations. The Lord hates wicked imaginations because He gave us a creative ability to use in His kingdom and to focus on what He instructs in the scriptures we have examined. If we learn how to sanctify, harness and use our imaginations for the purpose God intended, we could change the world around us. We could change everything about our lives. We could influence and change our cities and our nations.

18. discussion of young man focused on Adolf Hitler

Chapter Five Answers
Walking the Talk

1. Philippians 4:8 – *Finally, brethren, whatever things are true, whatever things are*
noble, whatever things are just, whatever things are pure, whatever things are
lovely, whatever things are of good report, if there is any virtue and if there is
anything praiseworthy—meditate on these things.

2. sanctified imagination

3. Word

4. practice

5. acceleration

6. practice

7. your paraphrase; ...those who practice their senses to discern good and evil

8. touch, taste, smell, sight, hearing, our sanctified imagination, and our logical
mind

9. Have you ever sensed the anointing? Have you walked into a room when two

people just had an argument? You didn"t hear it but you can *feel* that they just
argued. Have you been in a meeting where you have smelled the sweet fragrance of
a rose when you know there is no natural stimuli for such a scent? How is it that
you do that? That"s a supernatural phenomenon, but you"re engaging a natural
sense.
10. discussion and sharing your own personal literal "touch" from the Lord

11. God"s strength is made perfect in our weakness.
 2 Corinthians 12:9 - *And He said to me, "My grace is sufficient for you, for My*
strength is made perfect in weakness." Therefore most gladly I will rather boast
in my infirmities, that the power of Christ may rest upon me."

12. You can be the enemy of God in your imagination because you never harness it and use it for its intended purpose. The imagination is a creative tool in the hands of God. If you yield the creative tool of imagination to God and sanctify it, a whole new arena of possibility opens to you.

13. faith; works

14. We sanctify our imagination and put it to its intended use.

15. An anxious mind or imagination is always seeing defeat instead of victory, always seeing lack instead of abundance, always seeing sickness instead of health and healing, etc.

16. framed

17. wrath...
 Ephesians 2:1-3 ... *among whom also we all once conducted ourselves in the lusts of our flesh, fulfilling the desires of the flesh and of the mind, (imagination) and were by nature children of wrath, just as the others.)*

18. 1 Peter 1:13 – *Gird up the loins of your mind (imagination)*

19. Brother Lawrence

96
Study Guide Answers
20. Brother Lawrence practiced and practiced and practiced the presence of God. He set his heart and mind continually on the Most High all day long. Sometimes during his early years of exercising his sanctified imagination, his mind would wander for 15 or 20 minutes at a time. Each time, he would bring his thoughts back to the Lord and thank Him for His continued grace in disciplining His thought life. After a time, Brother Lawrence began to walk in profound revelation and intimacy with the Lord and the leaders of his day would come to him for counsel, for insight on the Word of God, and for understanding about who God was. He was developing such intimacy that it was noised abroad that Brother Lawrence knew God face-to-face, as a friend, just as Moses did.

21. yes!

22. exercise

23. group exercise

24. Exercising our senses by reason of use means we are going to have to practice and practice, and practice again, just like Brother Lawrence did!

25. Your answer: Yes or No. Some people might say, "Wait a minute, I''ve been interacting with the realm of the Spirit through prayer, and preaching and so on." No, I''m talking about a different level of maturity in Christ, of activation into the destiny that you have. What God is doing today, is allowing us to interact with the realm of the Spirit unlike any other generation that''s come before. What will happen as God''s people begin to walk in the fullness of this revelation, and we begin to model heaven on earth? What will happen when we begin to interact and walk in two realms simultaneously as mature sons and daughters of God?

26. Jesus Christ

27. The following scriptures validate visiting heaven.
2 Corinthians 12:2 Paul said: *I knew a man in Christ, whether in the body or out of the body, I don''t know. But such a one was caught up into the Third Heaven, and saw things that are not even lawful to express.*
In John 14:12 Jesus said, *The works that He does, we can do also, and greater works than these can we do because He has gone to the Father.*
Ephesians 2:6 *We are also seated together with Him right now in heavenly places. and*
raised us up together, and made us sit together in the heavenly places in Christ Jesus.

28. We have believed that doing the works Jesus did includes healing and casting out devils, and that we are to likewise do the same. Many have thought technology enabled us to be seen and heard by more people at the same time, for greater numbers, greater works, than Jesus reached at the same time. We have the privilege of doing the greater works because Jesus went to the Father. In examining the "works" of Jesus we can look at His life before He was resurrected and even after He was resurrected because He made no distinction. He didn''t say we would just do the works that He *"did"* before the Cross. He said, "The works that I *„do,"* you will do also." Right now He is at the right hand of the Father interceding for you and me at this moment.

29. Do not be discouraged if you were able to focus only a few seconds. Practice. Practice. Practice.

30. aiding

31. Discussion of portals. For those inexperienced in visions, consider prayer rooms or "holy places" you have been where you feel the peace of the Lord. These are also portals, even if you didn''t have a vision.

32. deception

33. Genesis 28 is the law of first mention of a portal. We are none other than the house of God, and the gateway of heaven. We can see the angels of God ascending and descending, and we can talk with Him face-to-face, just like Jacob.

34. flesh, price, unbelief, a religious spirit, and more

35. Practice focusing. One of the major obstacles to overcome is that most people can only focus on any one thing for no more than 12 or 13 seconds at a time before their mind begins to wander off. Close your eyes; frame a picture of Jesus, and focus. How long is it before your mind starts to wander? Continue this exercise several times a day throughout this course. Notice if your focus time increases. Record the results in a journal if that will help. At least record what you see in a journal.

36. Exercise on Ephesians 2:6 - *We are also seated together with Him right now in heavenly places. and raised us up together, and made us sit together in the heavenly places in Christ Jesus.*

37. It is important to communicate clearly with people. "Twitching fingers" is not a language people understand. Sometimes it''s best to just give the word, rather than how you arrived at receiving the word.

38. sanctify

39. *Metamorpho* means "to be transfigured; transform, change one''s form."

40. Follow Bruce''s instructions: "As I properly frame pictures of the Kingdom of God in my sanctified imagination, as I gaze into that mirror, I see Christ in me and myself in Christ. A transfiguration process begins as I become conformed to the image of Christ. Our ultimate destiny is to be totally conformed to His image and likeness. Your calling in life is to be conformed into His image. "Conformed" is the same Greek word for "transfigured," when Jesus was transfigured. We can attain total transfiguration through a renewed imagination."

Chapter Six Answers
The Living Body of Christ

1. prayer: All of you, Lord, and none of me

2. Discussion and application to pray this prayer for yourself daily.
Prayer
Lord, I want all of You and none of me. I want to be just like Jesus.

3. Discussion of Throne Room experience. Bruce"s answer to the extended scepter was "more of you, less of me" and Pastor Glenn"s answer was "whatever You want, Lord." Both answers are a complete absence of "our" agenda.

4. Yes, it"s ok to bring our petitions. It"s better to set aside our wants and desires for His.

5. Bruce learned that in this dispensation of time, the Lord is now bringing forth a generation whose sole passion will be to emulate and be like Jesus who was the mature Son of God.

He realized that what we deem significant and important is often not what the Father is passionate about. We must, however, be willing to set aside our wants and desires for His.
The expression "all of you and none of me" has to do with our character. We retain our personality because that is what makes us uniquely "us," but we lose our individuality. We become like Christ. We walk in Kingdom authority. We interact with the realm of the Spirit, and we become everything God says we are.

6. Discussion. The signet ring speaks of authority and coming of age in the family to which you belong. The moment you have the privilege of wearing that ring, you have the "backing of the house" to which that ring belongs. We are moving from a "give me" mentality to a "make me" reality!

7. Romans 6:13 paraphrase:
Do not present your members, your sense of seeing, smell, touch, hearing, tasting, as instruments of unrighteousness to sin, but present yourselves to God as being

alive from the dead, and your members, your sense of seeing, smell, touch, hearing, tasting, as instruments of righteousness to God.

8. personal prayer

Prayer

Lord, I sanctify my eyes and present them unto you as an instrument of righteousness. I sanctify my hearing, I sanctify my tongue, I sanctify my sense of smell, my touch, my imagination, my logical, reasoning mind. I yield them all to You today as instruments of righteousness.

9. You will keep him in perfect peace, whose imagination properly forms images of You, reflecting trust in You. The warfare we wage is not based on carnal weapons. The key is found in the admonition given us to *cast down imaginations and every high thing that exalts itself against the knowledge of God.*

10. purity

11. True

12. If you are born again and washed in the blood you have no past; you have a pure heart! Old things have passed away and ALL things have become new (2 Corinthians 5:17)! If I sinned, if I did something contrary to the Word of God 10 minutes ago, but have confessed and repented of that sin, I have a pure heart. The qualifier is the blood of Jesus.

13. No! The Bible doesn"t say "only" in heaven we will see God. You have pure hearts according to the Word of God and the washing of the Blood of the Lamb so you are qualified, and therefore you can see.

14. *Optanomai* means "to gaze at with wide open eyes, as if gazing at something remarkable."

15. optometrist

16. purity, grace

17. passion, fasting, prayer, and study of the Word

18. Discussion of the vision of Jesus in a pillar of fire.

19. love

20. Proverbs 23:26 – *My son, give me your heart, and let your eyes observe my ways.*

21. The heart connects with both the spirit and the soul. The heart is very hard to define even thought we say it is the mind (both the imagination and the logical reasoning faculty), will, and emotions. Everything you watch, hear, or see is burned onto the hard drive of your mind and begins to form who you are. If we don"t sort out what is right, what is wrong, what we"re supposed to think upon, what we"re supposed to speak about etc. we end up with a mixture. Everything we watch and see is burned onto the hard drive of our mind. That iswhy it is important for those who desire to move forward in God to sanctify their eyes, their ears and their mind. Taking responsibility for our thought life by applying the principles of the Word will sensitize us to the realm of the spirit. Without the sanctification of our thought life, we will continue on in a haphazard way in our spiritual progress. 103

22. True

23. True

Prayer
Father, I want of be a part of what you"re doing today.
(not bless me in what I"m doing today)

24. Psalms 16:8 - *I have set the Lord always before me.*
 2 Corinthians 3:18 - *But we all, with unveiled face, beholding as in a mirror the glory of the Lord, are being transformed into the same image from glory to glory, just as by the Spirit of the Lord.*
 Hebrews 12:2 - *...looking unto Jesus*
 Hebrews 11:27 - *...He (Moses) endured as seeing Him.*

25. The word "meditate" literally means to „utter silently under your breath, to chew on or to masticate." In other words, I"m going to mutter the scripture, I"m going to repeat it, I"m going to chew on it, I"m going to think about it so much so that it is going to become real to me. That is meditating on the Word. As I meditate on the word, I am framing pictures in my mind during the process.

26. "*We have borne the image of the man of dust, we shall also bare the image of the heavenly man*" means when you look in the mirror, you see your own reflection, but you"re told to see the Lord. In to 2 Corinthians 3:18, *Beholding as in*

a mirror the glory of the Lord, you are being transformed into the same image from glory to glory. As we learn to properly frame that picture of Jesus in us, somethinghappens. You begin to be changed and be transformed into His image.

27. transformation

28. Exercise gazing into the mirror, seeing Jesus. Beholding the Lord in yourself

will change you into the same image as you look and see the Lord in you. He is in your heart; you can behold the Lord in you. Build a bridge with your imagination because what you focus on, you connect with, and activation takes place.

29. darkened

Focus
Christ in me, the hope of glory

30. Enoch had a Christ-like character, nature, and integrity.
31. unbelief – If we truly believed the Word, we would live differently and act differently.

32. personal answer

33. seventh

34. personal answer

35. practice

36. The anointing in Bruce permeated and saturated the bed as he prayed and interceded every evening. The mother"s faith connected with that anointing and that is why her children were instantly healed.

37. Discussion of the anointing released on the massage therapist.

38. Exercise about radiating the anointing or Glory of God upon others.

39. clear

40. Matthew 6:21 - *For where your treasure is, there your heart will be also.*

Matthew 12:34 - ...*For out of the abundance of the heart the mouth speaks.*
Matthew 6:22-23 -

The lamp of the body is the eye. If therefore your eye is good, your whole body will be full of light. But if your eye is bad, your whole body will be full of darkness. If therefore the light that is in you is darkness, how great is that darkness!
23

41. Demons always reacted to Jesus. Anytime Jesus came into proximity with a demonized person, there was an instant reaction to Him.

42. Practice meditating on, imaging, and pursuing Jesus.

Chapter Seven Answers
Translation by Faith: Getting Ready

1. Translation means to be caught away physically, from one place to another.

2. True

3. Acts 8:39-40 is the New Testament account of translation.
 Acts 8:39-40 –
Now when they came up out of the water, the Spirit of the Lord caught Philip away, so that the eunuch saw him no more; and he went on his way rejoicing. But Philip was found at Azotus. And passing through, he preached in all the cities till he came to Caesarea.

4. We prepare to be translated --- by faith!

5. The Holy Spirit awakened Bruce one morning and asked, "Can a man be translated by faith?" Bruce answered, "Yes, I believe so." The Holy Spirit said, "Get ready." And more... the supernatural dream of a friend giving Bible references, the word from a friend about studying Isaiah again, his own experience, receiving the mantle to teach this revelation in two phases.

6. In the first phase, those being taught will be released and caught up into the Third Heaven. In the second phase, Bruce teaches how to physically translate like Phillip was translated so His Word shall be preached throughout the earth.

7. A Pastor in Russia ministers in three Churches ever Sunday morning. These churches are hundreds of kilometers apart.

107
8. Discussion on Richard"s translation, packing his bags and going to the airport, then worshipping God in the men"s room.

9. We are not the student"s of the Word that we should be, and we have difficulty believing that when the Lord says something we can "take it to the bank" because it is truth. Many have never had a supernatural experience and have been told that God no longer does these type things.

10. Jesus said in John 14:12 - *Most assuredly, I say to you, he who believes in Me, the*

works that I do he will do also; and greater works than these he will do, because I go to
My Father. Jesus made no distinction in his works before the resurrection or after the resurrection.

11. Discussion of Walking by Faith.

12. Prayer follows. (On Bruce"s website – stillwatersinternationalministries.com - are the DVDs of Brother Grubbs talking about his experiences.)
Prayer
Lord, if it is in Your Word, then I want it.
Whatever it is that You have, Lord, I want it.

13. Paraphrase of Jeremiah 29:11-13: You can have as much of God as you want; just be passionate about pursuing Him.
(Jeremiah 29:11-13 *For I know the thoughts that I think toward you, says the LORD,*
thoughts of peace and not of evil, to give you a future and a hope. Then you will call
upon Me and go and pray to Me, and I will listen to you. And you will seek Me and
find Me, when you search for Me with all your heart.)

14. The Holy Spirit will guide you into all truth and show you things to come. He only speaks what He hears.

15. Jesus said in I John 4:17b, ...*as He IS so are we in this world*, not ...*as He* WAS (when He was on earth), *so are we in this world.* Jesus IS in heaven with the Father now.
108
16. Discussion about the visit with Natalia

17. Discussion about the Chariot Rides

18. Out of the box discussion

Chapter Eight Answers
Translation by Faith: Going

1. Paraphrase: "This is what the Lord says. Stand at the road less trodden and discern. Earnestly desire the properly concealed vanishing point which is eternal and perpetual. Ask where the road less trodden is and journey and vanish in it and you will find rest for your souls."

2. "Old paths" means the road less trodden and refers to the ancient paths of scripture.

3. We must have discernment. Pursue God for it. We must believe God will give us what He told us to ask for. (Ask where the road less trodden is and journey and vanish in it.) It"s a place of rest, not a place of fear or striving.

4. Prayer follows.

Prayer
Lord, I ask for the ancient paths, the road less trodden,   so I can walk in them.
5. Discussion of Lesson One on translation

6. Practice being open to translation, in a shorter time taken for a trip. God is not limited by time.

7. The key of the house of David (Isaiah 22:22 -- the key of the House of David that you should open and no man can close and you can close and no man can open, the key of knowledge, and the key of the kingdom (which changed in shape and size depending on the situation.)

8. The purpose of the keys is to open doorways and portals.

9. We use a spiritual key by speaking the Word.

10. Uzziah represented pride. Pride has to die before we can see the Lord.

11. Unless we pay the price, we will not grow up into the fullness of Him. So paying the price results in growing into the fullness of Him.

12. Jesus became of no reputation. He was reviled and persecuted and yet He didn"t speak a word back to defend Himself. Jesus left the opulence of Heaven and took on the form of a servant.

13. Nazareth literally means "sanctification, separation, and crowning."

14. A good paraphrase is, "WOW! WOW! OH! WOW! because every time they turn around they see a new facet of the character of God they have never seen before throughout all of eternity.

15. The people of that generation knew that if they wanted to connect with or hear from the Lord, they should go to Shiloh and spend time, sleep, and dream so they could hear from God through a dream or vision. That was their normal way of communicating with God. We also need to set aside time to hear the Lord in a special place, and frequent that place expecting to see or hear.

16. thin (place)

17. Prayer follows.

Prayer
Grant that I walk in such a way so as to create the thin place
between heaven and earth.
112
18. personal application

19. Realize we have access to the supernatural realm and because of our new birth, are able to see in the Spirit. Embrace the Crucified life. If you make the choice, God will make the change because we are incapable in our own strength of entering into the fullness of the promise of God. So there has to be the release of the fulfillment of the Covenant, and the Covenant is just that – God"s strength replacing your strength. God"s resources for your lack, God"s understanding and wisdom for your lack of understanding and wisdom.

20. helper

21. servant

22. vanish

23. *yalak*

24. Isaac was 30-33 years old. He was not seen again until he met Rebecca, his bride.

25. A camel drinks 180-360 gallons of water.

26. Discussion of translation to Australia. He was worshipping when this experience happened.

27. change; able

Chapter Nine Answers
The Glory Within

Prayer

Father, activate this Word of *Gazing into Glory* in my life. Thank You, Lord, that You have chosen me as part of your Royal Priesthood at the end of the age, to show forth the goodness, the mercies, and the salvation of God throughout the nations. As I partake of this word Father, may I be filled to overflowing not just with the word, but with the Revelation of Your word that releases life. I pray, Father, that You would activate the angelic in my life. Release me, Father, to accomplish what You have sent me to do. I praise You, Father. One other thing, Lord -- the most important -- I apply the blood of Jesus over my life. This is seed that will not be snatched away in Jesus" Name. Amen.

1. clothed

2. a child dressed in mommy or daddy"s clothing, and completely hidden in them, except for their eyes

3. forethought

4. is

5. apply

6. mental; promise

7. If I truly believe, not just mentally agree, with the Word of God, my belief will be displayed in my thoughts, my words, and my actions.

8. The first example of a "work" is to prepare a place for Him. The second example is to allow the Spirit of God to reveal our own hearts to us. (John 14:12 tells us He prepares a place for us, and
9. Yes. We are seated with Christ in the heavenly realm and here in the natural realm at the same time.

10. wilderness

11. desolation and despair

12. by seeing the Lord face-to-face

13. Maybe we should change how we think about the wilderness. Most Christians don''t like the wilderness because it''s too tough. But that''s where we can meet God!

14. Paul gloried in tribulations because they brought him to more intimacy with the Lord. Seasons of brokenness, desolation, and despair purge and purify of your character.
Romans 5:3-4
And not only that, but we also glory in tribulations, knowing that tribulation produces perseverance; and perseverance, character; and character, hope.

4
15. disaster
(Without brokenness, pride sets us up for a fall.)

16. character

17. personal answer
The decision to do what God said was not based on logical reasoning about our ability (financial or otherwise) to obey Him.

18. Adam to Jesus was 4000 years (4 days), and Jesus to now is 2000 years (2 days). So we are in the morning of the 7th day (7000 years from Adam). God speaking from the cloud represents His presence or His Glory, which reverses the natural law of death and sickness. Today His presence, His Glory, is within us.
th

19. When the Glory was present, Moses just talked face-to-face with the Lord. He may have lived 1000 years, like Adam, because there is no death or decay in the Glory.

20. obedient

21. face-to-face

22. reverses
(This applies to anything touched by death, decay, and corruption.)

23. reasoning

24. dwelling
(It refers to the manifestation of the reddish-gold radiance of God''s presence

when it rests or dwells among His people on earth.)

25. because the Glory, among other places, is already in us
We need to release it from within ourselves.

Chapter Ten Answers
The Glory Released

1. He prayed silently and said, "Father, I release the Glory of God as my defense."
Prayer

2. canopy or defense

3. Mt. Zion; places

4. personal application

5. terror

6. blade

7. encase

I release the Glory of God as my defense.

8. The *huppa* of God"s Glory protects us from death, decay, and corruption.

9. Jesus walked in this world with no sickness and no disease inflicting him. When the religious people were going to throw Jesus off the cliff, the canopy of God"s Glory veiled Him, and He walked through their midst. They didn"t even see Him.

10. shade

11. H1N1 cannot get through the canopy of God"s Glory. Bullets cannot penetrate the Glory. Bombs cannot destroy it. Sickness and disease cannot penetrate it. Psalm 91 says we are under the shadow of His wing, with a thousand falling at your side and ten thousand at your right hand. It will not come near you. Famine is coming. We will pray over an empty pot at dinner time, and it will be filled with food! You"ll be able to say, "Come on in, Brothers, come on in, Folks." And they are going to ask, "How did you do that? Where did you get the food?" And you will share the reality of the Kingdom of God with them!

12. Our example of a mature son is Jesus. He walked in divine health, not needing healing.

13. By faith! Start with mosquitoes.

14. Discussion of releasing the Glory with regard to mosquitoes. Keep saying, "Father, I release the Glory."

15. Discussion of releasing the Glory with regard to aching teeth. Keep saying internally, "Father, I release the Glory."

16. ask God (and dialogue with Him)

17. Discussion of removal of mosquitoes from a family picnic. Release the Glory and let the family benefit!

18. The Glory gets rid of demons. They hate the Glory!

19. Discussion of no mosquitoes, healings, the suit staying new for seven years

20. sickness, sin, and death; Because He was made a curse for us.
Galatians 3:13 - *Christ hath redeemed us from the curse of the law, being made a curse for us: for it is written, Cursed is every one that hangs on a tree:*

21. radiance

22. envelope

120

23. meditation on the Glory within Jesus

24. meditation on the Glory within you

25. exercise of releasing the Glory
If you want to know Jesus face to face, practice releasing what is within you.

26. notched
(The Lord is a notched battlement and a shield or protector for us.)

27. discussion of Muslim village

28. Paraphrase of Isaiah 4:5-6: The Lord has created upon me as a dwelling place of
the Most High, a cloud and smoke by day which releases the terror and anger
of Yahweh against sinful man, but to me it is a mysterious wonderment,
attraction, reverence, joy, and confidence. There is a shining of a flaming fire by
night, this flashing of a sharply polished blade. For upon me the Glory is a

canopy that veils, encases, and protects. There is a covering, a protection from all heat, desolation, despair, and any instrument that would try to cut me down. It is a place of refuge and a secret hiding place from the storms of our enemy seeking to destroy me, and from distress and hardship.

29. Discussion. Bruce''s warning is to be led by the Spirit.

30. dream about the Glory being a shield and protecting us from bomb

31. See Appendix A.

32. Prayer from page 238 follows on the next page.

Prayer

Father, in the Name of Jesus, I thank You Your Word is true. We are in the Glory and the Glory is in us. Now, Father, by an act of our will, I am asking that You would fill us anew with the Holy Spirit and power, with an endowment of that Glory as we, by an act of our will, release that Glory. Right now, Father, all sickness, all disease, all death, decay, and corruption must leave our bodies in the Name of Jesus. Right now, the Zoe Life of God fills us anew! Now, Father, we release the Glory into our homes, into every corner, nook and cranny. All mildew, mold, decay, corruption, everything that is not life is eradicated out of this home in the Name of Jesus. Now, Father, we decree this is a place where Your Throne of Glory has free reign.

And we thank You, Father, that in the Glory there is no lack. Every need is met sovereignly, supernaturally, beyond our understanding, beyond what we could ask, think, reason or imagine. You meet every need because as He is - so are we in this world. Thank You, Father. Thank You, Father. Father, I am asking you right now, ratchet it up a notch.

Prophetic Word

It has been My Heart"s desire for many generations to raise up a generation that would yearn and long to know Me Face-To-Face, to move aside the religious blockade that has been placed between Me and My people. And this is the generation that I have chosen to know their God Face-to-Face. And so, I am releasing to this generation and to My people an understanding of My Word by the breath of Revelation that I release by My Spirit.

And I am releasing My people from chains that are not made by human hands, but that have been made by tradition and that have been made by human reasoning and that have kept you from the Kingdom of God. For I have chosen you in this generation to walk in the Courts of your King, to see that land that is far off, and to know your God in ways past generations never even imagined.

And I am stirring up within you a greater hunger and an understanding of the deep things, the secret things of the Most High. For you are a peculiar generation. You are a generation that shall see the fulfillment and the conclusion of the matter. You are a generation that has been chosen by Me to show forth the Praises of your God, and you shall do that by coming into the fullness of the stature of the knowledge of God whose you are.

And so I am saying to My people tonight, My Heart that has yearned for this moment is now being fulfilled because My desire is fulfilled. And in the days ahead, I will take you on an adventure in the realm of the Spirit beyond anything you could ask or think of -- beyond even reason or a comprehension of a carnal nature, but it will resonate within your spirit to such an extent because you are My children made in My image, created for My Glory, and you shall know My ways.

Also by Dr. Bruce D. Allen

Gazing Into Glory
Every Believer's Birthright to Walk in the Supernatural

Promise of the Third Day
Your Day of Destiny has Arrived

The Prophetic Promise of the Seventh Day
The Fulfillment of Every Covenant Promise

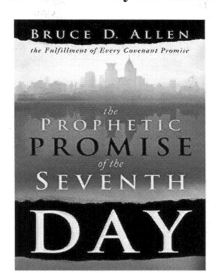

Books by Dr. Bruce D. Allen are available at Stillwaters International Ministries and at book stores and book distributors worldwide.